The Spirit and the Secular

The Spirit and the Secular

A Study of the Holy Spirit and Church Planting

PHILIP WILLIAM ZARNS
edited by Stephanie Leder
foreword by Anita Koeshall

WIPF & STOCK · Eugene, Oregon

THE SPIRIT AND THE SECULAR
A Study of the Holy Spirit and Church Planting

Copyright © 2021 Philip William Zarns. All rights reserved. Except for brief quotations in critical publications or reviews, no part of this book may be reproduced in any manner without prior written permission from the publisher. Write: Permissions, Wipf and Stock Publishers, 199 W. 8th Ave., Suite 3, Eugene, OR 97401.

All biblical citations, except where otherwise noted, are from The Holy Bible, New International Version®, NIV®, Copyright © 1973, 1978, 1984, 2011 by Biblica, Inc.™ Used by permission. All rights reserved worldwide.

Wipf & Stock
An Imprint of Wipf and Stock Publishers
199 W. 8th Ave., Suite 3
Eugene, OR 97401

www.wipfandstock.com

PAPERBACK ISBN: 978-1-7252-6915-6
HARDCOVER ISBN: 978-1-7252-6914-9
EBOOK ISBN: 978-1-7252-6916-3

03/31/21

This work is dedicated to women in ministry.
As you take on roles as pastors, apostles,
teachers, evangelists, and prophets,
know that we are better together.

Contents

List of Tables		ix
List of Figures		xi
Foreword by Anita Koeshall		xiii
Preface		xvii
Acknowledgments		xix
1	Introduction to the Problem	1
2	Biblical and Missiological Perspectives	9
3	Sociocultural Factors Affecting General Swedish Perception of Pneumatological Activity	38
4	A Historical Overview of Pingst Archival Literature of Their Perceptions of Pneumatological Activity Related to Church Multiplication	65
5	Field Research	93
6	A Theory of Pentecostal Church Multiplication among the Unchurched	123
Appendix A: Demographics of Respondents		141
Appendix B: Q Sort Concourse of Statements		144
Appendix C: Q Sort Concourse Sorted By Intersecting Dimensions		147
Appendix D: Q Sort Interview Instructions		151
Appendix E: Q Sort Target Grid and Interview		153
Appendix F: Q Sort Ideal Single-Factor Analysis		155
Appendix G: Q Sort Practiced Two-Factor Analysis		157

Appendix H: Q Sort Second-Order Analysis of Ideal, Practice 1, Practice   159

Appendix I: Consent Sent to Research Respondents   161

Bibliography   163

List of Tables

Table 1.1. The Pauline Cycle as Lived Out by Jesus in Luke's Gospel and Paul in the Book of Acts — 13

Table 5.1. Balanced in Engagement—Positive Responses — 103

Table 5.2. Balanced in Engagement—Negative Responses — 103

Table 5.3. Practical in Engagement—Positive Responses — 105

Table 5.4. Practical in Engagement—Negative Responses — 105

Table 5.5. Spiritual in Engagement—Positive Responses — 106

Table 5.6. Spiritual in Engagement—Negative Responses — 106

Table 5.7. Most Polarizing Statements — 108

Table 5.8. Summary Descriptors of Factors — 109

Table 5.9. Demographic Profiles of Factors of Factor 2, Factor 3, and Mixed — 110

Table 5.10. Second-Order Analysis Factor Matrix with Loadings Represented — 111

Table 5.11. Self-Recognized Movement between Q Sort 1, Ideal and Q Sort 2, Practiced — 113

Table 6.1. BiE Statements' Relational Direction and the Disciple/Church Multiplication Cycle — 134

Table 6.2. PiE Statements' Relational Direction and the Disciple/Church Multiplication Cycle — 135

Table 6.3. SiE Statements' Relational Direction and the Disciple/Church Multiplication Cycle — 136

List of Figures

Figure 1.1. Conceptual Flowchart of the Methodology   7

Figure 1.2. Conceptual Diagram of the Research   8

Figure 2.1. Disciple/Church Multiplication Cycle   26

Figure 2.2. Concentric Construction of Luke 19:1–7   36

Figure 5.1. Fisher's Balanced Block Design   95

Figure 5.2. Ideal, Practiced, and Future Values   120

Figure 6.1. Integration of Perspectives Informs a Theory of Pentecostal Church Multiplication   124

Figure 6.2. Spirit-Empowered, Balanced Approach to Planting Swedish Pentecostal Churches   127

Foreword

PHIL IS NO STRANGER to me. Long before Phil became one of my students, he and Katja arrived in Europe and joined the Students for Christ team that my husband, John, and I were leading. Assigned to Sweden, Phil and Katja settled in the Stockholm area and began reaching out to the students on the secular university—which led them to plant a church among young adults in partnership with the national Pentecostal church called *Pingst*. Besides his own church planting effort, Phil has watched as a number of church planting efforts have been attempted but have produced little fruit in comparison with the early growth in the *Pingst* movement at the beginning of the twentieth century. In light of their ten-plus years of work with one foot firmly planted in the secular Swedish culture and the other in a classic Pentecostal church, it's little wonder that Phil would choose to focus on the work of the Holy Spirit in planting churches among the unreached of Sweden.

Phil begins his study by tracing the massive changes that have taken place in Swedish culture: "Within one thousand years, the pendulum of faith has swung from pagan gods and human sacrifice, through Catholicism and Lutheranism, to atheism and the present postmodernity." "The disregard of theology, the prevalence of postmodern thought, and anthropological progression of secular culture has led to a regression of regard for supernatural activity in Sweden." He states that the prevalent mindset toward the supernatural is: "what you see is what you get," and a study of the present culture reveals that people have placed their faith in themselves and the secular humanist associations that populate Swedish society.

Phil postulates that this same mentality has seeped into and influenced the church, leading to the marginalization of the supernatural within the community of faith and a disbelief that "a divine being or force could interact with people to the point of constructing a favorable environment for humans to exist." Indeed, Phil and Katja found that the outworking of the cultural tendencies was evident in the new church they were planting. There, they experienced a dearth of Pentecostal expressions, which echoed the experience of other new church plants among Swedish young people. Phil began to question whether the decline in the reliance on the Holy Spirit to move and intervene in today's world was indeed hindering the lack of effectiveness experienced by the church planters. More specifically, did the church planters tend to rely more on activities that were typical in the culture to build an organization, such as networking or volunteering at non-profit organizations, rather than relying on prayer and fasting, the necessity of the baptism in the Holy Spirit, and mission?

Phil's inquiry took him from a biblical search of Luke-Acts on the work of the Spirit in church planting, to a historical overview of the rapid expansion and development of the Swedish Pentecostal church. Under the leadership of a powerful visionary, Lewi Pethrus, the church was planted across Sweden under the slogan, "one in every city." Pethrus relied on the Spirit for power for mission and evangelism but also challenged his churches to be invested in humanitarian efforts, especially during the periods of the World Wars. Obviously, Pethrus was not an either/or church planter. The interaction between the work of the Spirit and human effort worked in tandem to produce the church in Pethrus's day. Phil sought to find out if that is also true today.

Phil's relationships within the *Pingst* churches in Sweden made it possible for him to study the pastors' perceptions of the work of the Holy Spirit in regard to church planting. He conducted a Q sort with thirty of the forty-four *Pingst* church planters in Sweden, where the pastors ranked a variety of statements revealing their priorities: reliance on self-effort and practical elements; or reliance on explicit expressions of the Holy Spirit's activity, testimonies of miracles, and prayer and fasting more highly than practical considerations.

In their "ideal" sort—the way things ought to be—many of the pastors prioritized the work of the Spirit, but when they sorted the second time, indicating the way things actually were—the "real" sort—they ranked practical considerations higher. The comparison between their "ideal" sort and their "real" sort revealed a disparity between theory and praxis and drew them back to a place of reliance on the Holy Spirit.

Phil's work challenges all church planters to consider the extent to which culture blinds our eyes to the supernatural and inhibits us from trusting the Spirit to empower us to evangelize, disciple, and plant the church. Working through the pages of this book, you the reader may be curious to take the Q sort yourself and let it reveal your priorities, but whether you have that opportunity or not, may we all be challenged to understand the ways and times of our cultures, and then to engage the culture in the power of the Spirit to plant the church.

> Dr. Anita Koeshall
> Associate Professor of Intercultural Studies
> Assemblies of God Theological Seminary

Preface

THIS BOOK CONTAINS THE words of my dissertation. There will be moments where the terminology and writing style employed may easily be described as inaccessible. Please forgive me for those moments and, instead, consider the questions asked and the findings which follow. After you read, thumb through, search this document, take the opportunity for yourself to ask, "What does this study mean for future work?"

Pingst, the Swedish Pentecostal Church, began planting churches in Sweden in 1913 and continues to do so to this day. Church planters utilize a variety of approaches, yet none have been as effective as the method utilized at the outset of the denomination, when ministers united around the common goal of "one church per city." One church per city, *en församling i varje stad*, was a phrase first written by J. E. Forrest and used to inspire Holiness and Pentecostal movements to make disciples. In 1930, Lewi Pethrus elevated this idea and applied it to the cause of pioneering churches across Sweden.

As his vision was realized, Pethrus furthered the intangible catholic unity of the church to begin the fellowship of churches known as *Pingst*, the Swedish Pentecostal Church. As the movement developed, church planting began with larger cities as hubs and smaller towns as targeted outposts; churches were planted near the centers of each municipality. The apostolic expression of *Pingst* reflected the fervency of mission found at Azusa Street in its attempt to "try to get people saved."[1] The perceived theology and praxis of Pethrus during this period were closely related.

This research develops a theory of Pentecostal church multiplication by examining *Pingst* pastors' perceptions of the activity of the Holy Spirit in church multiplication among the unchurched. This research will investigate the perspectives of *Pingst* church leaders regarding the Holy Spirit from both historical literature and contemporary expressions. This research addresses the following objectives: (1) identifying the activity of the Holy

---

1. LaPoorta, *Globalization of Pentecostalism*, 35.

Spirit in church multiplication among the unchurched as found in Lukan/missiological literature, (2) identifying contextual factors that impact perceptions of church planting among the unchurched in the social location of Sweden, (3) identifying the perceptions held by the early *Pingst* pastors as recorded in the historical literature pertaining to the activity of the Holy Spirit in church multiplication among the unchurched, and (4) identifying the perceptions of *Pingst* pastors of the activity of the Holy Spirit in church multiplication among the unchurched. This study assists in identifying behaviors, attitudes, and values of *Pingst* leadership to inform future Pentecostal perception of the Holy Spirit in church multiplication among the unchurched.

The terms unchurched and unreached are used throughout this paper. My recent research, completed post-dissertation, leads me to question/disapprove of such words which utilize "un- + noun/adjective" as related to people and the church. Although based on an in-house, in-group ethnonym (churched, reached), negative syntax in social labels may cause unnecessary friction to the gospel being heard beyond such ascribed labels.

Acknowledgments

To write a dissertation takes time spent together with and apart from the people I love. There is no shortage of those people.

To my parents, thank you, Dad, for your work ethic, dedication to service, and multiple phone calls. Thank you, Mom, for your vocabulary, your endeavor to learn throughout time, and many messages. I am so glad you are my parents. Thank you for loving me.

To my in-law parents, thank you, Reijo, for your grace in pastoral work and for showing that a smile is always needed in this life. Thank you, Milja, for your kindness and for giving me your daughter's hand in marriage. From you both I learned that home can be found in multiple places.

To my big sister, Lisa, and brothers (in-law), Janne and Miika, thank you for the conversations—iron sharpens iron.

Thank you to Nicklas and Lydia Mörling, Pelle Hörnmark, and Daniel Alm for the opportunity to research and work as a part of *Pingst* in Sweden. Your kindness and open doors have allowed us to learn alongside your gracious examples of pastoral care.

To my fellow students in the ICS program, thank you for the time spent together in researching problems that are bigger than any earned degree. I hope to have a cup of coffee with you soon.

To my professors from the ICS program at AGTS: Paul Lewis, Alan Johnson, Mark Hausfeld, Beth Grant, Rob Gallagher, Charlie Self, John Easter, and Valerie and DeLonn Rance, thank you for sharing your lives, grace, guidance, and encouragement of critical thought when working through Scripture and culture. Thank you for loving both the student and the subject taught.

To my field research mentor, Bob Braswell, thank you for introducing me to Q method and the study of subjectivity in people. I am indebted to your dedication to integrating science with theological study. It's been a joy to talk about our shared love of guitars.

To the chair of my dissertation committee, Anita Koeshall, your academic rigor and example in ministry together with John truly inspires. I am forever thankful for your encouragement and dedication to refinement in academic response. Thank you for all of your work. I've learned much . . . including that you favor heavy cream in your coffee.

To my kids, Ben, Matilda, and Max, thank you for your care, fun, and laughter throughout this process. Each eye-to-eye conversation, impromptu trip to the lake to swim, and game of catch compelled me to finish this document, so we could do more of the like. Without you, this dissertation would not have been written. I love each of you—hugs and high fives!

Finally, thank you to my wife, friend, and partner in ministry, Katja. You have encouraged and supported this study through thick and thin, walking in grace alongside me, listening and reflecting back exactly what needed to be said. I have only learned more about your insight and care for me and others through your example. I love you. Coffee with you is the best.

1

Introduction to the Problem

As Katja and I left Sweden, we realized that our second church plant would face challenges as an organization. The church existed as a fellowship of believers and the unchurched. Concerns of leadership and venue plagued our minds as we pondered what we could have done differently to prepare the faith community for the future. Furthermore, expressions of the Spirit regularly occurring in other Pentecostal churches had occurred only a handful of times during the lifespan of the church. With practical and spiritual challenges facing the work, we consulted other church planters, finding that their churches faced similar situations. We wondered to what extent we were trusting the Holy Spirit while planting this church. Then, we questioned if the self-reliance of our expression of church planting could be considered Spirit-led. Conversely, was a focus on practicality in church planting removing a part of our identity as being Pentecostal?

BACKGROUND

Upon entering the new millennium, the Swedish Pentecostal denomination, *Pingst*, has faced digression in church fervency in comparison to the glory days of its early ecclesial renewal during the 1920s.[1] Their literature contains records of numeric success in church planting and foreign mission alongside a great emphasis placed on the work of the Holy Spirit in believers' lives.

---

1. *Pingst*—(Swedish) Pentecostal. *Pingst* is the adopted name of the Pentecostal denomination in Sweden.

2   The Spirit and the Secular

The greatest allusion to the days when Lewi Pethrus guided *Pingst* is the organizational style of church services, one leader speaking, while hundreds or thousands listen.[2] The homogenized, group-oriented societal structure of Sweden in the early 1900s provided fertile ground for the *Pingst* movement to grow through one cultural model for the newly formed Pentecostal church.[3] This singularity was catalyzed by leaders who implicitly and explicitly trusted in the Holy Spirit to inspire and lead the explosive growth among the newly planted churches in Sweden.

While working as missionaries to the Swedish people from 2007 to 2016, my wife, Katja, and I helped to establish university groups connected to local Swedish Pentecostal churches, as well as pioneered two faith communities in Stockholm. During this time, *Pingst* employed four different national approaches and/or methodologies to starting churches.

Proclaiming, gathering, developing, and sending believers into Sweden to plant churches that are contextually sensitive is of utmost importance, given the climate of secularity. *Pingst* displays an ability to adopt campaigns that complement their understanding of church structure. Equally, *Pingst* regards ministries not already in existence as implicitly unnecessary, providing little new place for those outside of the faith community.

The movement in Sweden began with the inspiration and sending of Spirit-empowered believers. Per their church planting director, Nicklas Mörling, without the leading of the Holy Spirit, *Pingst* would not have become a denomination of church-planting churches, let alone a single faith community.[4] Given the decreased efficacy of the movement in accomplishing church multiplication, questions about the reliance upon the Holy Spirit arise. Is the contemporary movement trusting in the Holy Spirit as their predecessors had? Could this be the reason why church plants are struggling? How can one go about investigating this occurrence?

This dissertation explores the research problem in the following order.

1. Biblical/Missiological research: Chapter 2 will examine Lukan and missiological literature in deriving the activity of the Holy Spirit as related to church multiplication among the unchurched. From this, the inspiration of the Holy Spirit is recorded in explicit action, with authors directly attributing the catalyst for church planting activity as the Holy Spirit.

---

2. Bundy, *Visions of Apostolic Mission*, 115.
3. Nida, *Customs and Cultures*, 38.
4. Mörling, interview.

2. Sociocultural: Chapter 3 seeks to understand the perception of pneumatological activity as explicit to Swedish culture.
3. Ecclesiological/Historical: Chapter 4 researches the historical perspective of the activity of the Holy Spirit related to church multiplication among the unchurched in Sweden based on archival literature.
4. Original Field Research: Chapters 5 and 6 research and analyze the ideal and practiced perspectives of *Pingst* pastors who have planted churches in the contemporary climate.
5. What does this all mean? In this final step we discuss what this research means to the future of church planting in a secular climate.

Unearthing historical and contemporary perceptions of the Holy Spirit is foundational for this research. The insights gleaned from the exegesis of Lukan literature (chapter 2) will assist in understanding the *lacuna*.[5] An exposition of Swedish culture (chapter 3) and consideration of *Pingst* church multiplication efforts from the birth of the denomination in the 1900s (chapter 4) will provide insight. Further, the field research focuses on discovering contemporary perceptions of the Holy Spirit in church multiplication among the unchurched (chapters 5 and 6). *Pingst* pastors ordered statements according to the parameters of importance and practice. The final step (chapter 7) integrates all the research findings into a unified theory of Pentecostal church multiplication by examining *Pingst* pastors' perceptions of the activity of the Holy Spirit in church multiplication among the unchurched.

PURPOSE

The purpose of this research is to develop a theory of Pentecostal church multiplication by examining *Pingst* pastors' perceptions of the activity of the Holy Spirit in church multiplication among the unchurched.

PROBLEM STATEMENT

What are the *Pingst* pastors' perceptions of the activity of the Holy Spirit that influence church multiplication among the unchurched?

---

5. A gap in knowledge.

RESEARCH QUESTIONS

1. What can be learned from Lukan and missiological literature about the activity of the Holy Spirit in church multiplication among the unchurched?
2. What sociocultural factors affect the general Swedish perception of the activity of the Holy Spirit in church multiplication among the unchurched?
3. What can be learned from *Pingst* archival materials about their foundational perceptions of the activity of the Holy Spirit in church multiplication among the unchurched?
4. In what ways do contemporary *Pingst* pastors perceive the activity of the Holy Spirit in church multiplication among the unchurched?

SIGNIFICANCE OF THE STUDY

The significance of this research will be as follows:

1. This study will relate God's call to faith communities to be empowered by the Holy Spirit, to exhibit awareness of his call to bear witness to the nations, and to become agile in adapting to their environment in contextualized forms with biblical functions. This research will inform present-day churches of theological and missiological understanding in regard to the activity of the Holy Spirit and to church multiplication.
2. A researched consideration of Sweden as social location will offer anthropological and sociological perspectives that may inform present-day American-European approaches to contextualization of church ministries.
3. This study will discover principles within historical *Pingst* documents that communicate past pneumatological interactions of the church. From this research, present-day Swedish church multiplication pastors may be informed of paradigm shifts in church culture and respond as followers of Jesus Christ.
4. This study will discover the present-day *Pingst* understanding of pneumatological activity as it relates to church multiplication. Considering a synthetic summary of the findings from the previous research questions, *Pingst* churches may be better informed and seek after the Holy Spirit's involvement in church multiplication endeavors.

GOALS

The subsequent outcomes of this study include the following:

- Presenting a description of multiplication as it pertains to Swedish Pentecostal churches by completing three tasks: (1) clarifying a theory as to how the activity of the Holy Spirit in Scripture and contemporary culture relate to church multiplication, (2) developing a theory of how culture affects church multiplication in Sweden, and (3) investigating the pneumatological activity within *Pingst* church multiplication as it relates to its past and present-day iterations.
- Describing factors that facilitate or hinder church multiplication in Sweden.
- Providing a theological framework to be employed in similar lands.

LIMITATIONS AND DELIMITATIONS

Limitations will include but not limited to the following considerations:

I attempt to interpret the data gathered through an objective lens, albeit Western, per my upbringing in Minnesota. It is assumed that those present during the early church multiplication of the *Pingst* movement in Sweden have passed on. In this case, the *Pingst* archives of church newsletters and correspondence will assist in the research. A foundational understanding of the Spirit as a catalyst will be attained from the documentation. I will attempt to glean the motivations and perceptions of the writers themselves through my interpretation of the events that occurred in *Pingst* history. Due to time and resource limitations, a Q sort study will be made according to availability of leadership. Access to local historical resources may be limited according to the quality and quantity of documentation provided.

Delimitations will include but not limited to the following considerations:

The activity of the Holy Spirit will be limited to explicit manifestations of interaction with humankind as found in Lukan and *Pingst* literature. No person could document the myriad of unperceived movements and inspiration that God initiates. For a focused gathering of information on the activity of the Holy Spirit, I will limit examinations of subjects to *Pingst* pastors who have experience in church planting in research question 4. Lay people will not be examined nor interviewed so as to provide control for the direction of research. Although the Swedish Lutheran Church is prevalent throughout Sweden and actively participate in the cultural development of Sweden in the past millennium, their clergy will not be interviewed. Yet their movement will inform research question 2 regarding the Swedish perception of *Pingst* church multiplication.

DEFINITIONS

A definition for each key term in the study is as follows:

> Assemblies of God (AG)—An American Pentecostal denomination formed in 1914 in the United States. A cooperative fellowship of ministers and congregations for the purpose of doctrinal integrity and common missional objectives.[6]
>
> Azusa—Relating to the spiritual awakening experienced through a series of meetings at the Azusa Street Mission in Los Angeles, California.[7]
>
> *Folkhem*—(Swed.—The People's Home) A concept begun in 1860 that centralized the political, social functions of the Swedish government. The removal of the church's power from healthcare and governmental systems accompanies this action.
>
> *Församling*—(Swed.—assembly)
>
> *Kyrkan*—(Swed.—church)
>
> *Pingst, Pingströrelsen*—(Swed.—Pentecostal) A Swedish Pentecostal denomination founded in 1915. This cooperative fellowship values following God and taking part in the mission of God as does its sister denomination, the Assemblies of God.
>
> PMU—*Pingstmission Utvecklingsarbete* (Swed.—Pentecostal Mission Development Work) The official branch of mission as connected to *Pingst*. Organized to provide opportunities for people to hear the gospel in foreign lands.
>
> Secularized—In reference to the removal of God and elevation of man in God's place. Traditions of the church continue to function yet with a diminishing view on the centrality of the gospel.

ASSUMPTIONS

The environment of Sweden grows more secularized with each passing year. Since the initial push to plant churches with the call of "one church

---

6. General Council, "History of the Assemblies of God."
7. LaPoorta, *Globalization of Pentecostalism*, 35.

per city," I assume that the *Pingst* ecclesial communities in Sweden have been affected by the environment they hope to reach. I assume a close relationship between the theory and practice of the early church regarding their understanding of the Holy Spirit and their church multiplication activities. I also hope to identify and categorize explicit forms of Holy Spirit activity as having influence in church planting efforts. My hope is to find a Spirit-led church within Scripture. This research will ascertain the validity of these assumptions.

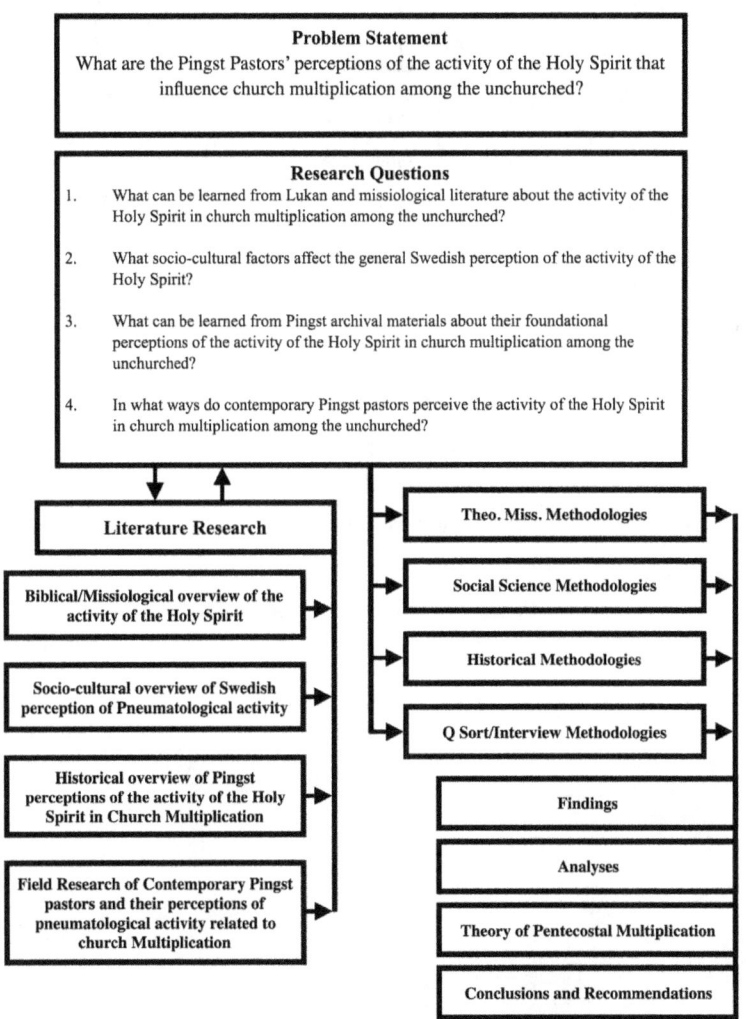

Conceptual Flow Chart of the Methodology

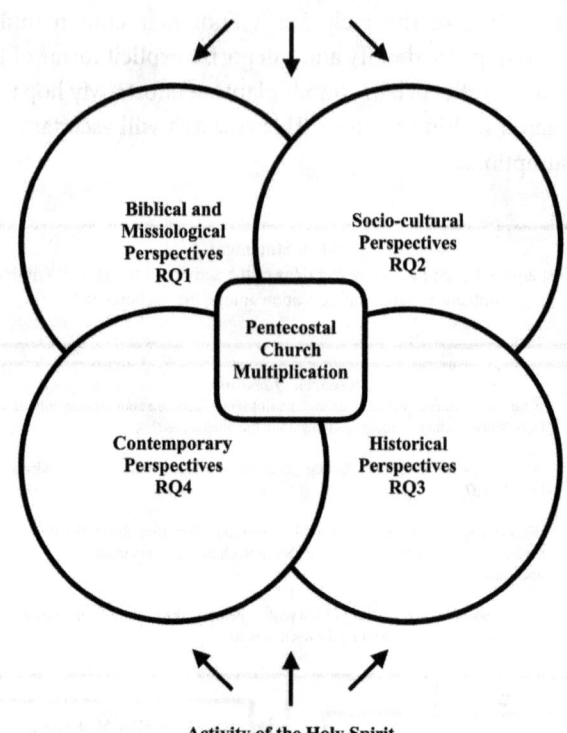

Conceptual Diagram of the Research

2

Biblical and Missiological Perspectives

THE ACTIVITY OF THE HOLY SPIRIT IN CHURCH MULTIPLICATION

In forming a theory of Pentecostal church multiplication, one must begin with biblical and trusted missiological sources to build a robust foundation of knowledge. The Gospel of Luke and the book of Acts, which bookend Christ's earthly presence, provides a seamless narrative between Christ's empowerment and Spirit-led work, as well as the formation of an empowered and Spirit-led church. Missiological authors who have researched and discovered motifs addressing this topic contribute to this research. Simply put, this chapter investigates Lukan and missiological perceptions of the activity of the Holy Spirit in church multiplication among the unchurched.

THE ACTIVITY OF THE HOLY SPIRIT DEFINED

In considering the Lukan understanding of the Holy Spirit, research is only possible through the examination of explicit movements of the Spirit.[1] The implicit inspiration of the Holy Spirit is relatively undiscernible apart from value-based assumptions derived from the presentation of biblical

---

1. Gallagher, *Mission in Acts*, 174.

personalities.[2] For the purpose of this research, the focus remains on the activity of the Holy Spirit surrounding events when the apostles/messengers engaged in the propagation of the gospel. The residual effects of this evangelization, as well as the further inspired actions of those empowered as colaborers alongside the initial apostles/messengers, are included in this study.

CHURCH OUTREACH/MULTIPLICATION DEFINED

Church multiplication refers to the general extension of the local church towards people unreached. Church outreach finds its identity in the authority and sending power of Christ (Matt 28:18–20). Certainly, multiplication involves making disciples, baptizing, and teaching them to observe and obey all that Christ taught. The act of making disciples involves the mentorship of all believers, including those experienced in and new to the faith. Baptism is understood as "the dawn of the rule of God in personal life and the common conversion to the future of that rule."[3] Populated by those who have placed their faith in his work on their behalf, the church of Jesus Christ provides an eschatological anticipation of "how things ought to be."[4] Contextualized faith communities, which share in *being* the church, strengthen the bonds between each member and God, as well as maintain integrity and care on a person-to-person level (Acts 2:42–45).

The propagation of churches is a function of evangelistic outreach per the writing of Melvin Hodges: "Paul stayed a limited time in one area, but he left behind a church that could govern itself, finance its own expenses, and extend the gospel throughout the region."[5]

Delivery of the gospel begins the gathering process for people to recognize their present situation and then future hope. The development of the church, then, requires that members assume roles in the building of the body, edifying each other in Christ. As a result, the autonomy of the church is a clear indicator that the people within the group are looking to God for provision as well to each other for whatever needs arise. Furthermore, Hodges emphasizes their opportunity to plant other churches. The cycle of planting a church arises from Scripture, founded on transmissions of leadership and truth found by people realizing Jesus Christ as center of their worship. A goal for contemporary local churches, which attempt to

---

2. Shaw and van Engen, *Communicating God's Word*, 140.
3. Moltmann, *Church in the Power*, 226.
4. Koeshall and Koeshall, "Ecclesiology-to-Go," 2.
5. Hodges, *Indigenous Church*, 4.

resemble biblical examples of healthy faith communities, is to proclaim the gospel, the seed of the church multiplication process.

METHODOLOGY

Data is collected by exploring biblical examples of pneumatological activity in relevant primary literature, including books and articles, as well as biblical studies, in order to discover how believers are purposefully sent by the Holy Spirit in church multiplication practice.

STRUCTURE TO DERIVE THE ACTIVITY OF THE HOLY SPIRIT IN LUKAN LITERATURE

In understanding Lukan connections between the Gospel of Luke and the book of Acts, attention should be given to the six-part structure of the two volumes. Most scholars conclude that the equal lengths of the scrolls onto which Luke and Acts were written could denote that these books are to be read in parallel or at least considered in light of one another.[6] While the structure of this outlook is dictated by the work of the Holy Spirit in action and direction, the explicit actions of Jesus Christ provide the structure by which to investigate the inspiration for each event. Jesus is the focus of the first three subsections based on what he did, taught, and left behind.[7] These three subsections focus on the being and doings of Jesus yet are driven to existence by the leading stimulus of the Holy Spirit.

The latter three parts to this structure focus on the disciples and their witness in Jerusalem, Judea, Samaria, and the ends of the earth. Again, the travels of the disciples provide the structure to Acts, which is rooted in their Spirit-empowered witness as explicitly explained in Acts 2. It cannot be overstated that Luke's understanding of the Holy Spirit, emphasized throughout his writing, encourages the inquiry of the reader, Theophilus, to provide his own pneumatological realizations.

PNEUMATOLOGICAL CATEGORIES AND SYNTHESIS

The Bible provides no systematic skeleton by which one can understand all of his functionality, yet narrative theology provides a way to realize categories

---

6. Keener, *Acts*, 1:554.
7. Gallagher and Hertig, *Mission in Acts*, 11.

of God's interaction through the Spirit.[8] Explicit references to the Holy Spirit as found in Lukan literature denote (but not limited to) the Spirit's personal presence (e.g., Luke 1:35), communication of future events (e.g., Acts 11:28), as well as operative guidance (e.g., Acts 10:19–20). Each characteristic of the Holy Spirit provides clues into the involvement and orchestration of God in the founding of his church through people open to allowing him to use them for his purposes. These categories find interpretation in their connection to humanity. The inspiration of the Holy Spirit alongside a believer's obedience causes God's will to come into being. God's Spirit communes with Jesus in the "union of divine essence and human nature."[9]

God's translation of himself through events found in Lukan literature establishes a possibility for connection with each person. God communicates through creation, the prophets, through "mighty" acts, through Jesus, through the Holy Spirit, and then through his people.[10] Viewing these few attributes of the Holy Spirit in a holistic manner allows the reader of Luke and Acts to synthesize a perspective of the Holy Spirit as having a faithful, guiding presence.[11] The key motive of the Holy Spirit is to transform and empower people by leading them to the central hermeneutic of life, Jesus Christ crucified, risen, and exalted.[12] His faithful, guiding presence is evidenced in Lukan literature in believers who experienced the baptism in the Holy Spirit and became compelled to partake in church outreach, which led to church multiplication.

PAULINE CYCLE OF CHURCH MULTIPLICATION

A diversified representation of how to understand church outreach and multiplication originated in David Hesselgrave's Pauline Cycle.[13] As events arise from Lukan literature, categorizing them under the motif of church multiplication steers the reader to consider the process involved in the globalization of the church. The cycle begins with the origination of a Spirit-empowered missionary sent into another culture to begin the process. This is embodied by Jesus and realized by the primitive church. The Holy Spirit enables the church to engage the surrounding cultures. Perhaps this cycle is misrepresented in being called the Pauline Cycle as it was first

8. Kärkkäinen, *Pneumatology*, 23.
9. Kärkkäinen, *Holy Spirit*, 69.
10. Gilliland, *Word Among Us*, 156.
11. Hunter, *To Change the World*, 241.
12. Lingenfelter, *Transforming Culture*, 17.
13. Hesselgrave et al., *Planting Churches Cross-Culturally*, 58.

presented by the sole individual to display such a sharing of God's power, Jesus Christ.[14] The example of the primitive church as Spirit-empowered communicates to the contemporary audience of Lukan literature that the Spirit is the author of the church. As a result of his inspiration, subsequent churches are birthed.[15] The Spirit catalyzes the movement of people to meet as a community of faith, which is why the development of a Pentecostal theory of church multiplication is necessary.

Table 1.1. The Pauline Cycle as Lived Out by Jesus in Luke's Gospel and Paul in the Book of Acts

	Jesus—Luke	Paul—Acts
Missionaries Commissioned	Luke 10:1–23 Jesus commissions the seventy-two	Acts 13:1–4 Spirit through leadership commissions Barnabas and Saul
Audience Contacted	Luke 6:17–19 Multicultural crowd gathered	Acts 13:14–16 Multicultural crowd gathered
Gospel Communicated	Luke 7:50 "Your faith has saved you"	Acts 13:17 "God delivered Israel"
Hearers Convened	Luke 21:37, 38 Disciples follow Jesus	Acts 13:48 Believers assembled
Believers Congregated	Luke 22:14–19 Last Supper	Acts 13:43 The devout followed
Faith Confirmed	Luke 24:52, 53 "They worshipped him . . ."	Acts 14:21 A number of disciples won
Leadership Consecrated	Luke 5:1–11 Jesus calls the first disciples	Acts 14:23 Appointed elders to churches
Believers Commended	Luke 10:38–42 Mary and Martha	Acts 16:40 Encouraged Lydia
Relationships Continued	Luke 24:36 Jesus appears to the disciples	Acts 15:36 Revisiting disciples
Sending Churches Convened	Luke 24:51 Jesus returning to his father	Acts 14:26 Return to Antioch

14. Malina, *New Testament World*, 61.
15. Wenk, *Community-Forming Power*, 266.

While the life of Jesus is not chronologically aligned with the Pauline Cycle, the leading of the Holy Spirit confirms that the inspired actions of Jesus lead to the beginning of the primary faith community. The groundwork in revealing the roles of Jesus as Messiah, Redeemer, and Savior within the Gospel of Luke is the foundation for the Pauline Cycle. Lukan literature reveals an unwavering need to rely upon the Holy Spirit prior to and throughout the process of church multiplication.[16]

Jesus as Spirit-Led in Church Outreach in Luke

Luke's narrative of the involvement of the Holy Spirit in church multiplication spans the works of the Gospel of Luke and the book of Acts. The conception of empowerment and guidance of Jesus Christ creates what today's people realize as the contemporary church. These called-out sinners find the centrality of Jesus as the point of repentance (Luke 5:32).[17] As a direct result of the Spirit's work in Jesus Christ, lives are transformed. Investigation of key events from the life of Jesus assists in understanding what it means for believers to be led by the Spirit in life and ministry.

Baptism

Explicit action follows the inspiration of the Holy Spirit in most of Luke and Acts; however, the initial giving of the Holy Spirit from the Father to the Son provides evidence as to where the Spirit originates. A clear display of this relationship can be found in the baptism of Jesus Christ by John the Baptist (Luke 3:22). In this instance, the preparation of Jesus as one who "proclaims good news to the poor" includes the Holy Spirit descending from heaven and resting on him in the way that a dove would descend (Isa 61:1–2). Jesus's ministry began when the Holy Spirit was imparted to him (Luke 3:23).[18]

Two voices spoke out about Jesus Christ regarding and during baptism: John the Baptist offered testimony about Jesus's way of baptizing, and God's own voice spoke as authentication for his Son. Each had qualified Jesus as one who held spiritual power found in his relationship to God the Father.[19]

---

16. Allen, *Missionary Methods*, 9.

17. All Scripture quotations are from the 2011 New International Version unless otherwise specified.

18. Stronstad, *Charismatic Theology of St. Luke*, loc. 995.

19. Childress, *Opening Up Luke's Gospel*, Luke 3:21–22.

Holy Spirit as Guide

Pinnock describes the Spirit as "guiding, luring, wooing, influencing, drawing all humanity, not just the church."[20] Humanity returns to God through the exertions of the Holy Spirit. Post-baptism, Jesus is led by the Spirit into the wilderness to be tempted by the devil. From this encounter readers learn from Luke that (1) the Spirit leads a Spirit-filled Jesus into a situation that can be considered perilous, and (2) difficulties can be navigated by the guidance of the Holy Spirit. While a reader cannot derive the implicit movements of the Holy Spirit within Jesus, the following verse demonstrates and confirms the infilling of the Spirit after the encounter in the wilderness: "Jesus returned to Galilee in the power of the Spirit, and news about him spread through the whole countryside" (Luke 4:14).

In Luke 4:14, Jesus returns to Galilee in the "power of the Spirit." This reference highlights the implicit prophetic guidance of the Spirit prompting Jesus. His very direction and geographic placement are inspired by this pneumatological guidance. In a parallel manner, Jesus's own empowerment immediately preceded his inspired preaching as it would in the Spirit-empowered primitive church to come (Acts 4:15, 18).[21]

In the latter chapters of Luke, the Holy Spirit provides joy to Jesus, which then leads to praise of God (Luke 10:21). Through examination, the effects of the internal pneumatic unction experienced by Jesus lead to externally perceived events. In this case, an emotion catalyzed by the Spirit, leads to proclamation and worship. Furthermore, Jesus emphasizes that the Holy Spirit is given by God the Father, interconnecting those who receive this Spirit, so they receive the possibility to be prompted to worship God themselves. The empowerment and guidance of Jesus Christ by the Holy Spirit is accessible to all.

While guided by the Holy Spirit, Jesus Christ then instructs the disciples to wait for the "power" that God had promised to his people (Luke 24:49). The guidance afforded to Jesus, and in turn given to Christ's followers, helps them to carry on what he had started. While the Great Commission is situated in the Gospel of Matthew, Luke's treatment at the close of his Gospel provides an accentuation on the transference of the Holy Spirit to the disciples and fellow followers of Jesus in Acts 2. David Bosch notes that this passage encapsulates Luke's entire understanding of the Christian church outreach.[22] What took place between Jesus and his disciples would

---

20. Kärkkäinen, *Pneumatology*, 142.
21. R. Menzies, *Empowered for Witness*, 144.
22. Bosch, *Transforming Mission*, loc. 10044.

then also occur from the apostles to the early church, and so forth. This process included both proclamation (kerygmatic) and assistance (paracletic) as the Spirit helps humans to pray and live.[23]

To the Unchurched: The Jewish People

The Jewish people had long been considered to be God's chosen to bring a message of salvation to the ends of the earth (Exod 6:7), though Luke traces the paternal lineage of Jesus, "so it was thought," through Adam to God himself (Luke 3:23–38). This connection recognizes God's salvation for all people through Jesus, who was born through the Jewish nation. This salvation and sovereignty that originated from God would extend divine law into "all the areas of life."[24]

Jesus's way of living for God diverged from the Pharisees and the Sadducees in the orthopathy and orthopraxy that followed their interpretations of the Law.[25] Jesus presents a new way of understanding the Law and the Law fulfilled. Furthermore, Jesus's way of living is compelled by the Holy Spirit, who leads towards the possibility of salvation for all (Luke 24:46–47). Thus, Jesus sought to proclaim, gather, develop, and send Jewish people into the world to proclaim the day of salvation to God's chosen and beyond (Luke 19:9; Isa 56:7). Given the Western propensity to default towards a process based in causality and events, God graciously allows humans to piece together ways of understanding his nature through theology.[26] This action of constructing a theology assists the hearer of the Gospel of Luke and book of Acts to find themselves as participants in the story of God and to accept the commission given to the original disciples. Within the Gospel of Luke, Jesus narrates God's movements and characteristics by modeling and inviting others to participate in the *missio Dei* themselves.[27]

SENDING

The very act of God sending Jesus to dwell on earth was the ultimate sending motion of the Father to his creation, from divinity to humanity.

---

23. A. S. Anderson, *When You Come Together*, 66.
24. Sanders, *Judaism: Practice and Belief*, 191.
25. Orthopathy—correct experience or passion; orthodoxy—officially "right glory" or commonly "right belief"; orthopraxy—right action.
26. Bosch, *Transforming Mission*, 261.
27. Webber, *Narrate the World*, 122.

This action is considered to be cross-cultural based on the culture of God and the culture of humankind.[28] Once symbiotic in reliance upon God, the relationship of creation to the Father drastically changed in Genesis 3. The empowered incarnation of God in Jesus Christ coming to earth is to be interpreted as God's intention to evangelize and disciple his own people (Luke 1:29–37).

As Jesus lives out his earthly ministry to humans, he shares wisdom, power, and authority. The sending motion of God would not be singularly found in Jesus but would be shared with his followers. Initially, he shares with the twelve disciples his power and authority to "drive out demons and to cure diseases" (Luke 9:1–2). Central to *missio Dei*, the shared, sending motion of God is found in verse 2, where the disciples are to proclaim the kingdom of God and to heal the sick. In the following chapter of the Gospel of Luke, Jesus sends out seventy-two disciples ahead of his travels to do as the previous twelve had done.

Proclaiming

After being led by the Holy Spirit into the wilderness, Jesus returned to Galilee in the power of the Spirit. In turn, the Spirit compels those with whom he communes and inhabits towards mission. This compelling nature of God implies the movement and transference of information from one culture to another. Jesus embodies the role of change agent in prompting groupings of people to not only shift their behavior but also to shift their focus of worship.

Jesus's task of proclaiming the kingdom of God and curing the sick is shared with coworkers, furthering the reach of God (Luke 9:6). The total dependence upon God fueled their travels as they performed what Jesus modeled for them. As commissioned change agents, they proclaimed and healed just as Jesus had before them.[29]

As a precursor to the works to come, Jesus speaks of God's favor in Luke 4:18–19: "The Spirit of the Lord is on me, because he has anointed me to proclaim good news to the poor. He has sent me to proclaim freedom for the prisoners and recovery of sight for the blind, to set the oppressed free, to proclaim the year of the Lord's favor." In order of Jesus's reiteration of Isaiah 61:1–2, the Spirit precedes the proclamation of the good news, the freedom of prisoners, the healing of the blind, the right standing of the oppressed, and the proclamation of God's favor. As proclamation of

---

28. Grunlan and Mayers, *Cultural Anthropology*, 21.
29. Arrington and Stronstad, *Full Life Bible Commentary*, 439.

the gospel bookends and the healings and freedom experienced, Jesus fulfilled God's plan of action in creating faith within the Jewish nation.[30] His statement about himself as the Savior-Redeemer as communicated by Isaiah was accompanied by a warning about the way the Jewish people would not receive him. Jesus stated that the widow of Sidon and Naaman the Syrian had received assistance; then he juxtaposed these instances with the ill acceptance of the prophets of old as well as himself.[31] Reception of God's Spirit-empowered sent ones who proclaim the good news accompanied by healings and freedom is of key interest to God. If the Jews would not receive him, then the Gentiles would.

Jesus extends a similar idea in the proclamation of the twelve and the seventy-two disciples. If the disciples would abide alongside, the recipients of their message would depend on the hospitality extended or withheld to the disciples (Luke 9:5). The disciples continued moving from town to town under the power and authority afforded them by Jesus (Luke 4:43). Proclamation, then, can have two outcomes: (1) the recipient of the message can find joy in the news, be healed, and enjoy the company of the bearers, or (2) the recipient of the message can find the news to be lacking in goodness, continue in a broken lifestyle, and displace the bearers of the message.[32]

Gathering

Following the proclamation, Luke shows the crowds gatherings and those who wished to retain a higher level of devotion following Jesus than to view Jesus as a spectacle. Scripture denotes large gatherings of people (Luke 4:40; 5:1; 6:17; 7:1; 8:4; 9:10; 12:1). Luke provides treatment for calling and gathering of the twelve disciples (Luke 5:11, 5; 6:12–16; 11:1). These disciples would be sent to partake in the Disciple/Church Multiplication Cycle. Their work would follow in the footsteps and Spirit-empowered witness of God's good news, accompanied by the healing of the inner person as well as the outer.[33]

---

30. Smith, *Major Prophets*, 61.
31. Arrington and Stronstad, *Full Life Bible Commentary*, 413.
32. Childress, *Opening Up Luke's Gospel*, 4:31–44.
33. Fee, *Paul, Spirit, People of God*, loc. 2533.

Developing

Jesus endeavors to help the disciples to better understand his sovereignty and teachings.[34] His lessons spanned from communicating to God the Father, to walking by the guidance of the Spirit, to the realization of the kingdom of God and Jesus as the key to understanding it all.[35]

On sovereignty, Luke divulges the culmination of the internal assertions of the disciples through Jesus's questioning of Peter (Luke 9:18–20): "Who do you say I am?" This question posed by Jesus implies that Peter is to make a judgment on who Jesus is and of what consequence it may have for him. As a Jewish person, Peter reveals that Jesus fits the description of the coming King, "God's Messiah." This Savior would change the way that future generations would regard God. Peter reveals his own theological repentance through learning and applying God's good news to his present reality.[36] Correction, which originates from reflection on who Jesus Christ is and how believers are to react as Spirit-empowered disciples, is of the utmost importance in making disciples and growing future churches.

The Early Faith Community as Spirit-Led in Church Outreach in Acts

Luke brings into focus the transference of God's Spirit into the budding church through his writing in the Acts of the Apostles, which reveals the Holy Spirit as the primary catalyst of church multiplication. As a result of Jesus Christ's Spirit-empowered witness, his disciples began to display parallel when he sent them. They proclaimed the good news, gathered people, and developed them in further realizing Christ's lordship through all of their being. While following their unfolding revelation about who Christ was to them, the body of Christ became known as a group of people who continued in the *missio Dei* that Jesus embodied.[37]

To the Unchurched: The Gentiles

While Jesus shared his message of salvation to the Jewish people, his actions communicated that he simultaneously included the Gentiles in his plan of salvation. Foreshadowed by the singular inclusion of the very recipient of

---

34. Carson, *Christ and Culture Revisited*, 53.
35. Moltmann, *Church in the Power of the Spirit*, 67.
36. Anderson, *Ministry on the Fireline*, 208.
37. Luzbetak, *Church and Cultures*, 119.

the Gospel of Luke and the book of Acts, Theophilus, the "loved-by-God," was almost certainly a Gentile.[38] Additionally, Isaiah foretold the gospel of salvation to the Gentiles: "It is too small a thing for you to be my servant to restore the tribes of Jacob and bring back those of Israel I have kept. I will also make you a light for the Gentiles, that my salvation may reach to the ends of the earth" (Isa 49:6).

Further, at the close of the Gospel of Luke, Jesus helped the disciples to understand what was to occur next after his ascension:

> Then he opened their minds, so they could understand the Scriptures. He told them, "This is what is written: The Messiah will suffer and rise from the dead on the third day, and repentance for the forgiveness of sins will be preached in his name to all nations, beginning at Jerusalem. You are witnesses of these things. I am going to send you what my Father has promised; but stay in the city until you have been clothed with power from on high." (Luke 24:45–49)

The disciples would tell Jesus's story to all nations, beginning at Jerusalem. The addition of the Greek word *de* (translated as "but") provides a provision that they must stay in Jerusalem until they had received the Spirit-empowerment that he had as well.[39] The importance of this passage and its counterpart in Acts 1:8 is displayed throughout the book of Acts.

Baptism

The book of Acts continues the narrative of the Holy Spirit interacting with humankind by revealing the baptism in the Holy Spirit through an event consisting of several elements of transformation. The evidence of God's connection to humans in Acts 2 displays the external sign of tongues and fire floating above people's heads as God baptized each one. Simultaneously, the foundational recognition that those baptized received power for service was evident to those present. In the opening of the book, Luke recounts the words of Jesus Christ regarding the Holy Spirit's commitment to empower the church in the New Covenant (Acts 1:8).[40] This didactic segment enables the reader to understand the emphasis of this empowerment through Luke's listing of reminders.[41] First, in Acts 1:2, the reader is reminded that Jesus

---

38. Keener, *Acts*, 1:659.
39. Thomas, *Hebrew-Aramaic and Greek Dictionaries*, 1161.
40. Peterson, *Acts of the Apostles*, 129.
41. Miller, *Empowered for Global Mission*, loc. 405.

himself instructed the disciples "through the Holy Spirit," foreshadowing Acts 12:10. Secondly, the instruction is given in verse 5 for the disciples to wait in a location for what was promised from God the Father. This *epangelia*, promise, connects Jesus's words before his ascension together with the understanding of the inheritance of Israel to be a blessing.[42] Thirdly, the baptism in the Holy Spirit is named and juxtaposed against John's baptism with water. While the repentance of John's baptism is valid, focus is placed on the transformational moment where water and Spirit are present.[43] The focus on transformation following baptism foreshadows the outreach Paul accomplishes in Acts 19:1–7 with the twelve disciples in Ephesus unaware of the Holy Spirit. Verse 8 culminates this recapitulation of Jesus's teaching on the Holy Spirit and provides a scriptural base for the latter part of the six-part structure of the book of Acts.[44]

The events of Acts 2 encapsulate the movement of the visible impartation of the promised Holy Spirit and the movement of the disciples in evangelism from Jerusalem to the world. The feast of Pentecost was a celebration of harvest, an occasion to announce that God was Lord of the land, and by grace he would bring forth food to the people.[45] Through the incredible symbolism offered through this Hebraic lens, God was performing outreach into the nations by first contracting groups of Jews from all over the region.[46] As Jesus was sent to proclaim the good news, so the church would be sent as well.[47]

This harvest of people through the Pentecostal experience, however, would not be kept to the Jewish peoples, but it soon would become generous in both geographic reach and cultural diversity. The bounded sociological set of Jewish people who had viewed themselves as the sole recipients of the promise of Abraham was about to shift. The Jewish people would soon need to acknowledge that Jesus could become the center of not only their religion, but of a faith available to all. The centered set with Christ as the middle point of pilgrimage would be realized in Acts 10.[48]

---

42. Keener, *Acts*, 1:21.
43. Loder, *Transforming Moment*, 94.
44. Gallagher and Hertig, *Mission in Acts*, 13.
45. Sanders, *Judaism: Practice and Belief*, 139.
46. Gallagher, *Acts: Course Manual*, 112.
47. Cowdell, *Is Jesus Unique?*, 143.
48. Hiebert, *Conversion, Culture and Cognitive Categories*, 8.

The Spirit and the Secular

Holy Spirit as Guide

The person of the Holy Spirit is emphasized in Luke 12:10 as one who can be addressed through blessing and cursing by humans. Luke adds to Theophilus's dimensional understanding of guidance and interaction with the Holy Spirit. In an unrelated discourse regarding the arrest and prosecution of believers, the Holy Spirit teaches them through his guidance. The hearers of Jesus's teaching would have understood how Israel had cried out for a king in the place of reliance upon their unseen God. The shift from reliance upon the incarnation of Jesus Christ towards the unseen Holy Spirit, then, would not have come as a surprise to the disciples (Acts 12:12). What Jesus did in the early parts of the six-part structure of Acts was prepare the disciples for how they themselves could rely upon the Holy Spirit as displayed in the book of Acts.[49]

Sending

In these Lukan passages, Jesus primarily instructs and embodies the path of a person entirely led by the Holy Spirit. The fruit of these efforts results in glorifying the Father in heaven, bringing attention to him through action. The Holy Spirit promised empowerment for service in Luke 24:49, giving life to the new faith community; the Spirit would lead them in leading Jesus Christ.[50] Through the account of Acts 2, different languages were uttered by the Spirit-empowered disciples and understood by those crowding around in the open air. Those who heard their own tongues being spoken inevitably asked, "What does this mean?" (Acts 2:12). In consideration of the book of Acts, Theophilus would realize the extension of the empowerment of the Spirit to the disciples and potentially to himself.

Proclaiming

The account of Acts 2 has the speech that the newly Spirit-empowered Peter boldly shared. It is noteworthy that Peter's earlier status as a disciple was one of shame (Luke 22:62). The empowerment of the Spirit provided a supernatural confidence to Peter and the eleven standing with Peter as he offered his discourse as to why this event was occurring. He contextualized his message according to the recipients, citing King David and Scripture

---

49. Childress, *Opening Up Luke's Gospel*, 11; Gallagher and Hertig, *Mission in Acts*, 23.
50. Menzies, *Empowered for Witness*, 32.

from the prophet Joel. Even Jesus's placement of Jerusalem as the center of sending would assist Peter in knowing his audience as he tailored words born of the Spirit.[51] Throughout the book of Acts, proclamation of Jesus Christ is shaped to be understood and received by the hearer.

In Acts 4:8, Peter and John are brought to trial before the rulers, elders, and Pharisees. This passage displays the prophetic gravity of Jesus's connection to the Holy Spirit as he once warned in Luke 12:11. Their reliance on the Holy Spirit at the time of trial assists them in sharing the core of their evangelistic message, the good news of Jesus Christ (Acts 4:12). This example of outreach is not a present reality in Western civilization, yet the applicability of one's reliance upon the Holy Spirit to any situation will only build in trust in the reliability of God's faithful presence.[52]

Further on in Acts 6, seven disciples are commissioned to replace the twelve apostles in the serving of the people on a daily, practical basis.[53] Of the Greek-speaking disciples chosen, Stephen is named as one who is "full of the Holy Spirit," denoting his character, source of guidance, and countenance.[54] After this passage, another scene follows in which Stephen is brought before the Sanhedrin, where he would be judged in a similar fashion to what Peter and John had experienced, and of course, how Jesus said he would be judged.

This developing theme shows the dependence upon the Holy Spirit as an integral part in the delivery of the gospel in these difficult situations. Acts 7 tells the story of the martyrdom of Stephen, in which he fulfills the great commandment as a witness who produces a record of his faith in Jesus Christ, guaranteeing the historicity of the major events in his Savior's life.[55] Whereas the assumed result of being placed into trial for one's faith and then relying on the Holy Spirit for deliverance may not give that result in a grounded, earthly sense, the release through bodily death towards an eternal life with Jesus Christ is certainly a reward in itself (Acts 1:8).

Acts 8 shares two key encounters, one in which Philip meets a sorcerer who wants to purchase the power of the Holy Spirit and, conversely, the other in which a God-fearing Ethiopian servant travels to the court in his home country. Placing these examples of etic interest in the things of God, the apostle must decide how to qualify their desires. Philip performed signs and wonders to the people under the power of the Holy Spirit, which gained

51. Bauckham, *Bible and Mission*, 66.
52. Hunter, *To Change the World*, 241.
53. Fernando, *Acts*, 244.
54. Horton, *Acts*, 137.
55. Peterson, *Acts of the Apostles*, 112.

the attention of an audience to hear the good news of Jesus Christ. It is noteworthy that Philip did not control the Holy Spirit but instead yielded to the guidance and prophetic power of the Spirit for the use of outreach, edification, and encouragement per Peter's words in Acts 4:29–31. Philip's work is the fulfillment of the prayer from that time, moving forward in sharing public testimony of who Jesus Christ really was.[56] The sorcerer looking on exhibited traits of his own adherence to the concept of an in-group.[57] Simon the sorcerer wanted to integrate God's power into his own plethora of powers and actions. The Ethiopian, however, did not look for such an audience but asked how he as a member of an out-group could be transformed to be a follower of Christ based on the information of the gospel being shared with him.

The outreach displayed in these two situations reveals the potential for the message of Jesus Christ to change the course of people's lives based on their humility. Certainly, these stories demonstrate a difference in the status of each of their hearts and the asymmetry of their structures of understanding.[58] The results of these encounters show that while one reevaluates his motives in trusting Christ, the other finds allegiance to God.[59] Seeds produced fruit where they met fertile ground.

Acts 9 presents the cornerstone of orchestration of the Holy Spirit in the lives of two individuals. God speaks to both Ananias and Paul so that their paths might cross in Damascus. While Saul bears witness to the death of Stephen at the close of Acts 7, Luke foreshadows his contribution to the evangelization of Jerusalem, Judea, Samaria, and the ends of the earth. The Holy Spirit guides Ananias to a specific place to visit where he greets Paul and states that he will pray for his healing and that he will be "filled with the Holy Spirit" (Acts 9:17). This example of Ananias and Paul displays how one person filled with the Holy Spirit can pray for another to be filled with the Holy Spirit as well. The cognitive journey that Saul traveled in the salvation experience challenged his very being. Yet, if he could have falsified his experience, little to no transformative lifestyle would have followed.

Jesus confronts Saul, asking him to consider his future Lord.[60] Saul, filled with the Holy Spirit, instructs and teaches all that Jesus had taught the disciples. Paul's transforming moment altered his mind to be renewed and to continually consider the mind of Christ as his own (Rom 12:2). This would

---

56. Fitzmyer, *Acts of the Apostles*, 311.
57. Rogers and Steinfatt, *Intercultural Communication*, 49.
58. Koeshall, *Redeemed Power*, 243.
59. Kraft and Gilliland, *Appropriate Christianity*, 100.
60. Loder, *Transforming Moment*, 24.

allow him to navigate the Sanhedrin as Peter, John, and Stephen had done to bear witness to the gospel. He would traverse a path not unlike Moses's, where he once was a slave to sin (Rom 6:20). He had experienced anarchy in his own soul against God by adhering hatefully to the Law (Gal 4:8–9). He would experience equity in his understanding of being a coheir with Christ alongside brothers and sisters in God's family, and then he would find a way to express his inclusion into *missio Dei* through God-honoring structured hierarchy, and he would send other Spirit-empowered believers into the harvest.[61]

Gathering

Early in the book of Acts, those baptized in the Holy Spirit came into close proximity with the visiting Jewish people (Acts 2:14). The Jews wondered why the disciples were speaking in languages that they recognized. Peter confirmed this occurrence in conjunction with proclaiming the gospel. As a result of that encounter authored by the Holy Spirit, three thousand heard the good news of Jesus Christ and responded in devotion (Acts 2:42–45). As the disciples engaged the cultures around them, each grouping of people would hold differing dynamics. One-on-one meetings, as in the example of Philip and the Ethiopian (Gentile), formed a dyad that would represent that of the learned and the curious (Acts 8:34). Certain gatherings were intimate where Gentile God-fearers had requested information from an apostle, as in the example of Peter in Capernaum (Acts 10). Paul gathered smaller groupings of people through the proclamation of the gospel (Acts 16:14). Even when encountering difficulties in Philippi alongside their meeting with Lydia, the inspiration of the Holy Spirit would be evident in their songs, sung from the prison cell. From this experience, the jailer himself sought after salvation after the sign of the earthquake (Luke 16:30–31).

Developing

The remainder of the book of Acts recounts Paul's visits to the interior of Asia, Greece, and his encounters with various cultures, which he would engage through the power of the Holy Spirit.[62] Each place that he preached would yield a small or large grouping of disciples. Through revisiting those places where he had evangelized, Paul sought to form leadership that would consider

---

61. Wildavsky, *Nursing Father*, 25.
62. Costas, *Christ Outside the Gate*, 89.

the work of Christ as outlined in Matthew 28:18–20, again, teaching all about the good news of the Messiah by relating his own story.[63] The salvation and commissioning of Dionysus and Damaris in Acts 17:34 demonstrates that Gentiles and Jews would have access to hearing about Jesus. Dionysius became the first bishop to send missionaries out from Athens, a place known for their pluralistic tendencies as a culture.[64] Further, Paul's meeting with Jewish believers in Ephesus who had taken on the repentance that John the Baptist had preached would end with twelve disciples realizing mission and being full of the Holy Spirit (Acts 19:6). The Holy Spirit interacted with the disciples by sending them to establish faith communities.

A PENTECOSTAL THEORY DISCIPLE/ CHURCH MULTIPLICATION CYCLE

The interaction of the Holy Spirit with humankind through the ministry of Jesus Christ from the Gospel of Luke and the resulting disciples in the book of Acts can be categorized as the acts of proclaiming, gathering, developing, and sending, which will be referred to as the Disciple/Church Multiplication Cycle. Broad categories drawn from Scripture provide a foundation for a Pentecostal theory of church multiplication. The granular perspective of the Pauline Cycle informs this cycle as well.

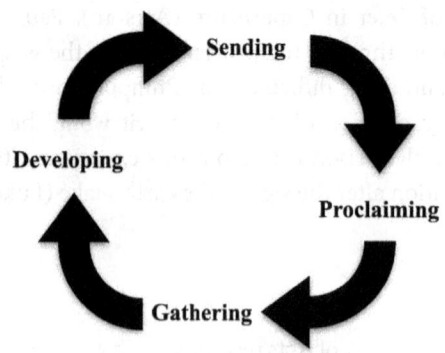

Disciple/Church Multiplication Cycle

---

63. LaPoorta, *Globalization of Pentecostalism*, 157.
64. Peterson, *Acts of the Apostles*, 504.

Exegetical Exercise: Paul and the Disciple/Church Multiplication Cycle to the Unchurched

Of germane interest to this research is Paul's interaction with secular culture, characteristic of Sweden's own self-descriptive boast.[65] Within the environment of Athens, a plethora of perspectives on spirituality coexisted. Paul's meeting with the leaders of Athens displays the efficiency of the gospel amidst pluralists.

Developing: Paul

Paul confidently trusts in Christ with his calling. Reliant upon the Holy Spirit while in dire circumstance, Paul was proficient in languages, argumentation, and in his approaches to both Jewish and Gentile cultures.[66] Being multilingual was not uncommon in New Testament times; Paul either employed translators or presumably spoke *Koine* Greek, Aramaic, Hebrew, and Latin.[67] Born in Tarsus, within the Roman Empire, Paul favored the Pharisaic perspective of Jewish practice from a young age. His harsh actions towards Christians, however, did not reflect the multicultural tolerance nor compassion that his primary teacher, Gamaliel, was known for.[68] Upon encountering Jesus Christ, Saul experienced a shift in the allegiance of his faith. On the other side of his decision, a community of believers assisted him in changing his earlier lifestyle bent towards staunch Judaism towards embracing his multicultural heritage and using his Greek name, Paul.

Sending: Paul

Attribution to his change in allegiance is found in his encounter with Ananias:

> Then Ananias went to the house and entered it. Placing his hands onto Saul, he said, "Brother Saul, the Lord—Jesus, who appeared to you on the road as you were coming here—*has sent me so that you may see again and be filled with the Holy Spirit.*" Immediately, something like scales fell from Saul's eyes, and he

---

65. Swedish Institute, "10 Fundamentals of Religion in Sweden."
66. Van Rheenen, *Missions*, 171.
67. Porter, *Paul: Jew, Greek, and Roman*, 305.
68. Miller, *People and Places in Scripture*, 121.

could see again. He got up and was baptized, and after taking some food, he regained his strength. (Luke 9:17–19, italics mine)

Working from his now redeemed, Spirit-led perspective on life and ministry, Paul realized the opportunity to evangelize Gentiles. As a young man, Paul was educated as a Pharisee. His newfound zeal to understand Jesus of Nazareth as the Messiah far outshined his past attempts at holiness.

His written voice reveals the pain of his past success in working towards fulfillment of the Law. The grace that God showed Paul granted him freedom from this regret, yet the residue of his emotions certainly motivated his writing to help others who may relate to his previously misguided efforts.

At the time of the writing of Paul's letters, the recent and far-past experiences of his life had culminated in one of two situations. His sorrow that he had been misguided in his spiritual endeavors may have driven him to depression. Paul exhibited a drive not unlike his stint in hunting Christians while "breathing out murderous threats" (Acts 9:1). This new chapter of his life in Christ still contained his characteristic fervor.[69] The expression he had was a motivated outworking of joy, employing his salvation to share Christ through his own weakness and strength.

Applying the psychology of Erik Erikson to Paul's rebirth experience in Christ, or anyone's experience for that matter, would be the reapplication of the famous stage "identity vs. role confusion."[70] Although this stage of development is normally reserved for adolescents, Jesus tells us that that alignment with him produces a regenerative effect (Eph 2:10). His reidentification through the Holy Spirit results in an integrative repurposing of one's time and priorities.[71] His new identity would use the same drive to share the message of salvation about Jesus the Christ, regardless of culture.

Paul in Athens (Acts 17:16–34)

The urban center of Athens presented the challenge of a pluralistic culture invested in multiple idols.[72] Fleeing a relentless Thessalonian crowd who pushed him out from Berea, Paul found himself waiting for Timothy and Silas in Athens.

This city was not only one of three academic epicenters of Greece, but it enjoyed the protection of the Roman government and did not pay taxes to

---

69. Erikson and Erikson, *Life Cycle Completed*, loc. 1291.
70.. Erikson and Erikson, *Life Cycle Completed*, loc. 825.
71. Loder, *Transforming Moment*, 128.
72. Fitzmyer, *Acts of the Apostles*, 604.

Caesar.[73] True to his zealous apostolic calling, he "was enraged" at the idolatrous adornment of the city, which would soon inform his culturally congruent oratory method to deliver the gospel.[74] The implicit leading of the Spirit finds him unashamed to share the gospel in a pluralistic setting. It was said of the city that it was easier to find a god than to find a man.[75] Paul began his kerygmatic duties within the synagogue, reasoning with the expected Jewish and Greek God-fearing audience in the hopes of catching men.[76]

Proclaiming: Paul

Paul continued his mandate of proclamation to the Roman Agora (marketplace), which sharply contrasted with the homogeny of the synagogue in creed and ethos. Paul was met in debate by pluralistic Stoics and pleasure-seeking Epicureans, who could not understand his advocacy for Christ (Acts 17:18).

Stoics maintained rationality as a framework of thought, striving to live in harmony with nature. They attempted to remove all cultural and national boundaries from their identity, bestowing equal rights of citizenship within their pantheistic theology.[77] Further, the Stoics were known to prefer logic, physics, and ethics as subjects of debate and teaching, for their general perception of humankind was that all people possessed the power to be good within themselves.[78]

Epicureans claimed rationality and sought after self-fulfillment.[79] They were known for avoiding excess material possessions and for accentuating the importance of low-impact living. Tranquility in one's surroundings and within oneself was of utmost importance. Any outside philosophical construct that did not emphasize that ultimate authority was grounded in a humanistic thought was considered false, according to the Epicurean.[80] Paul's kerygmatic preaching produced deeper inquiry by the diverse onlookers. His commitment to persuasion gained the audience of the chief council of Athens, the Areopagus (Acts 17:4).

---

73. Peterson, *Acts of the Apostles*, 488.
74. Horton, *Acts*, 412.
75. Easton, *Bible Dictionary*.
76. Newbigin, *Gospel in a Pluralist Society*, loc. 1622.
77. Bruce, *Book of Acts*, 330.
78. Peterson, *Acts of the Apostles*, 490.
79. Horton, *Acts*, 413.
80. Arrington and Stronstad, *Full LIfe Bible Commentary*, 627.

The Areopagitican Discourse

The governance of the Areopagus sought to discern the meaning of Paul's illuminated message, as the judges of both law and spoken presentation for the Athenian community. The place of council sat perched atop a high outcropping of white marbled rock, promising not only a prominence to its task of devising justice but its importance as separate to the multipurpose existence of the Parthenon temple.[81] Paul was undoubtedly aware of the heritage of the Areopagus, which had been known for centuries to be primarily used in prior times for the adjudication of homicides.[82]

Understanding and tolerating the religious structure around him—although he found it heretical, to be sure—Paul opened the discourse by referring to the unknown God, using the altar that inhabited their surroundings as revealing his attributes in respect to the men of Athens. Paul's environment supplied a highly contextualized backdrop to his message, hoping to deliver a clear connection between humankind and the deity in question. As a culturally aware apostle, his experience and training helped him to avoid both condescending reductionism through the use of simplistic language as well as adding too much information that would simply lead to confusion. He encoded the gospel so that their seasoned ears might understand the gravity of his message (Acts 17:21).[83] Citing the creative, generative nature of God to the Epicureans and his timing to the chronologically minded Stoics, Paul focused on God's sovereign nature in creating order to life itself. That this deity was separate from their existence did not collide with Areopagus' understanding of their present orientation to the divine. The turn arose as Paul alluded to the kingdom of God and the proximity of the unknown God as being "not far," and that "in" him they live and possess life (Acts 17:27–28).[84] He crescendos his appeal by quoting from the poets Epimenides[85] and Aratus,[86] using their understanding as offspring of Zeus.[87] Paul appealed to the artistic expression of the Athenian leadership, utilizing the vehicle of poetry to soften the landing of Jesus's resurrection and humankind's place in it.

---

81. Swanson and Nave, *Topical Bible*, Parthenon Temple.
82. Keener, *Acts*, 3:2601.
83. Hiebert, *Transforming Worldviews*, loc. 4033.
84. Kistemaker, *Exposition of the Acts*, 637.
85. "in thee we live and are moved, and have our being." *Cretica*.
86. "in every way we have all to do with Zeus, for we are truly his offspring." *Phenomena*.
87. Kistemaker, *Exposition of the Acts*, 636.

Paul continued to cleverly use their logic to create a faith directed towards God that would result in repentance. He then delivers the crux of his presentation to the audience.[88] Although it is possible that the entire discourse is recorded in Scripture, Paul exhibits patience with each delivery of the gospel, taking time to share the message well. His patience for the response to the truth he shares would have a limit, however. Paul then shares that the one responsible for true justice was embodied in a resurrected man. Further, this man would not answer to the public forum of the Areopagus but rather them to him. Paul's presentation was one that displayed a personal, rather than an impersonal, God. It bears mentioning that Paul does not mention the name of Jesus Christ in this discourse.

The Areopagites were caught in a crisis of belief that led to reactions of either distaste or of trust.[89] The point of conflict within their minds was that an unseen Creator had interacted with *their* earth.[90] Their placement of themselves as the center of the universe, as the ultimate authority in the workings of theology, had been compromised. The primary action of Paul was to proclaim the gospel of Jesus Christ, a task that he discharged with precision. This would lead to the inclusion, empowerment, and sending of Athenians to share in the *missio Dei*.[91] As a missionary, Paul sought those who had not heard the name of Jesus, Jew and Gentile alike (Acts 2:39). His egalitarian understanding of the grace of God's reach and sending power had resulted in him being ejected from sharing amongst Jews in a previous encounter.[92]

Gathering: Paul

Paul endeavored to utilize the asymmetrical power structure of the Areopagus, so God might redeem those within.[93] Dionysus, one of the council members, desired to hear more of this unknown God. As he was named after the Greek god of wine and revelry, it would be as if today he were named Jack Daniels. Dionysius would serve as the first bishop in Athens,[94] according to tradition, living out a reidentification much like what

---

88. Arrington and Stronstad, *Full Life Bible Commentary*, 627.
89. Kraft and Kraft, *Christianity in Culture*, loc. 1752.
90. Horton, *Acts*, 425.
91. Newbigin, *Gospel in a Pluralist Society*, loc. 2561.
92. York, *Missions in the Age of the Spirit*, 87.
93. Koeshall, *Redeemed Power*, 229.
94. Eusebius, *Ecclesiastical History*, 85.

Paul experienced through his salvation and empowerment.[95] A prominent woman, Damaris, also experienced the fruit of the gospel. Paul continued planting churches where none existed; however, there was no record or letter connected to an Athenian fellowship.[96] The letter written to the church at Rome does seem fitting for this new faith community as Paul accentuated the equality that is found within the family of Christ (Rom 8:16–17; 10:12–13).

Summary of Paul's Church Multiplication Cycle to the Unchurched

Paul's awareness of his apostolic mission led some to follow a previously unknown gracious and compassionate God, further revealing the fulfillment of the promise once made to Abraham.[97] The gospel was dispensed cross-culturally and with the precision afforded by one powered by God's Holy Spirit to disciple *panta ta ethne*.[98] As a result of God's Spirit compelling Paul, faith communities were started by proclamation of the gospel regardless of the context.[99]

Paul in Ephesus (Acts 19:1–7)

"The baptism in the Holy Spirit is not a separate event from salvation, it happens at the moment of trusting Christ" (*Pingst*, 2015). These words, uttered by a Swedish Pentecostal pastor to hundreds during the annual Pentecostal Pastor's Conference in Stockholm 2015, elicited a gray response from the crowd.[100] Some nodded in understanding, while others tilted their heads to the side, questioning the words of the pastor. This statement would challenge the very foundation of the Pentecostal movement, likening their denomination to other Free Church movements that maintain the idea that the spiritual distinctive of Spirit-baptism is not rooted in subsequence but occurs at salvation. Relating to the contemporary topic at hand, Paul's encounter with disciples at Ephesus who had not experienced the Holy Spirit interjects perspective into this discussion. Acts 19:1–7 offers a didactic

---

95. Bruce, *Book of Acts*, 343.
96. Johnson, *Apostolic Function*, 72; Horton, *Acts*, 425.
97. York, *Missions in the Age of the Spirit*, 86.
98. Gk.—to all nations.
99. Mittelstadt, *Reading Luke–Acts*, 157.
100. Elmer, *Cross-Cultural Connections*, loc. 149.

segment worth noting for its continuance of the precedential baptism of the Holy Spirit throughout the book of Acts.

Context of Acts 19:1–7

Ephesus was known for being a marketplace hub for the Silk Road trade, as a pagan worship hotspot given the massive temple of Artemis, and as a multicultural conglomeration of peoples.[101] An important element of ancient cities like Ephesus was a high degree of transience within the population. As a result, introduction of new ideas in the agora of the city was a regular occurrence. Paul can be understood, much like Jesus, to have preached to Jewish people within the synagogues, and to both Jews and Gentiles in group-oriented, ruralized city settings.[102] Paul is aware of the contexts in which he travels, trusting that the baptism in the Holy Spirit would compel disciples to be sent in mission, just as Barnabas, Silas, and Paul were sent after their own encounters.[103] Paul situates his visit to Ephesus as a transient himself, after visiting the churches of South Galatia, which were established on his first missionary journey.[104]

Paul's encounters with pagan followers would soon include those who revered Artemis, the sister of Apollo. Whereas the temple had been destroyed twice beforehand around 300–200 BCE, the ruins of the temple would continue to inspire sacred prostitution based on hopes of fertility for those who partook in the festivities.[105] The instruction of Apollo's contemporary would be a foreshadowing of the instruction of Artemis's idolaters in the following chapter. Regardless of the foundational philosophy of the culture in Ephesus, Paul carried a transformational message to the disciples he found on his path.

Paul's Proclamation and Gathering the Twelve

Mirroring the previous chapter's encounter between Priscilla and Aquila, who instructed Apollos about Christianity to a great extent, Paul had his own opportunity in Ephesus to instruct twelve disciples who had not received the Holy Spirit (Acts 19:2). Apollos may have only been preaching

---

101. Gallagher and Hertig, *Mission in Acts*, 249.
102. Allen, *Missionary Methods*, 60.
103. Stronstad, *Charismatic Theology of St. Luke*, loc. 1602.
104. Horton, *Acts*, 449.
105. Keener, *Acts*, 3:2871.

the baptism of repentance, revealing his baptism in the tradition of John the Baptist to be useful yet not complete (Acts 19:3). Upon consulting the audience of Paul's address, the presence of twelve disciples was ignored as insignificant by some scholars. The multicultural setting finds a parallel in the apostles' experience in Jerusalem in Acts 2.[106]

The narrative endeavor of Luke draws a distinct line of connection between the participation of Jews, leading to a diaspora of Christian belief within their networks, and the participation, now, of Gentiles who would similarly contribute to the evangelization of Asia (Acts 19:10). The Holy Spirit sends believers to proclaim the gospel, which then gathers, develops, and sends people into mission as like-Spirited messengers.

The Holy Spirit's Developing and Sending of the Twelve

Missio Dei is the assigned concept that mission is the "sending of the Son . . . with an inclusive aim of establishing the lordship of Christ over the whole redeemed creation."[107] The word *inclusive* here pertains to the inclusion of people as those to be used in the effort to continue what had begun in Genesis 15 with Abraham in each setting of culture, contextualized with innovation to the culture with fidelity to biblical Scripture.[108] Acts 19:1–7 shows an audience who had not yet realized the lordship of Jesus Christ nor the empowerment for service through the baptism in the Holy Spirit (Acts 19:6). Paul then finds himself in the company of those who had not heard of how one might receive the Holy Spirit. The building blocks of starting a church are found in this passage. Paul is sent to make disciples, teach (*kerygma*) those pre-disciples of Jesus Christ, baptize them in the name of Jesus Christ, and then pray about their reception of the Holy Spirit. Per the Church/Disciple Multiplication cycle, the gospel is proclaimed, people are gathered, developed, and inevitably sent by the Spirit for service.[109] Paul and Luke clearly had a process of how a person could engage in similar behavior, enacting their role within *missio Dei*. As a result of this process and multiple participants to grow the budding faith community, churches are planted.[110]

---

106. Keener, *Acts*, 3:2824.
107. Engelsviken, ="Missio Dei," 482.
108. Dowsett, *Global Mission Church*, 11.
109. Hesselgrave et al., *Planting Churches Cross-Culturally*, 58.
110. York, *Missions in the Age of the Spirit*, loc. 3817.

Pentecostal Empowerment in Acts 19:1–7

Truly, the idea of subsequence as related to the baptism in the Holy Spirit is a theological question rooted in how humans understand God's empowerment of those who by faith trust in Jesus Christ as their Savior. In the writing of Luke, however, special attention is paid to presenting the repentance of a person in the following example of water baptism (Acts 19:4–5). Another phrase is written to express a differing event from the moment of baptism in water. Paul then places his hands on those who have been baptized in the name of Jesus Christ, and what happens next is the baptism in the Holy Spirit. The development of disciples to be sent relies on the baptism in the Holy Spirit to occur in a believer's life, according to Paul's example in this passage. In the recording of Scripture, Luke utilizes stories of cause and effect to relate his theology to Theophilus, yet these stories unfold in the covering of history so as to avoid the argument of whether these events actually happened.[111] Luke delivers information through writings of subsequence, with the understanding of the literary devices that would bring understanding to a reader that two events are happening at the same time.[112] The Greek word *hama* is used to express simultaneous phenomena within the book of Acts, while in the case of the epistles of Romans and Colossians, *hama* expresses the sociological grouping of people together.[113] Given two occurrences of *hama* in Acts, one may construe the reality that two separate events of purpose are happening in a sequential order. Both a surface and deep exposition of this passage conclude empowerment for service from the Divine Giver.[114]

Taking into consideration the context and function of this passage, the underpinning of the baptism in the Holy Spirit as an empowerment for service serves as a catalyst for missional fission.[115] In verse 1 of Acts 19, Paul's path through the interior of Asia along trade routes culminates at a terminus, an urban center such as Ephesus, where he could reach the populous because change is normal.[116] Paul's missionary methods utilized the order of the culture to communicate Christ, as in the example of Athens in Acts 17. Per a review of Roland Allen's interpretation of Pauline church planting, the ordered, and albeit "myopic," understanding of these methods

---

111. Miller, *Empowered for Global Mission*, 405; Keener, *3 Crucial Questions*, 188.
112. At the same time—*hama* (Gk.), Acts 24:26
113. Peterson, *Acts of the Apostles*, 642; Strong, *Concordance*, loc. 15492.
114. Menzies, *Empowered for Witness*, 234.
115. Nunes, *Wittenberg Meets the World*, 105.
116. Hesselgrave et al., *Planting Churches Cross-Culturally*, 97.

left little room for church propagation outside of a Lone Ranger, maverick mentality that would "seize the culture."[117]

Acts 19 makes it clear that the Ephesians presented an opportunity for Paul to continue and realize the spread of the gospel. Verse 2 begins with a question Paul posed to the disciples whom he found in Ephesus. He asks about the Holy Spirit along with their proposed ignorance of his presence. Verse 3 reveals Paul's assumption of the disciples being baptized. There must have been something about the appearance, behavior, and demeanor of the disciples that brought about Paul's inquiry of baptism. The assumption is that they were repentant at their core. Since the culture of Ephesus was pluralistic, it should be of no surprise to the reader that there were disciples present were aware of baptism through John the Baptist.

Verse 4 presents not only the dissemination of Paul's charge to preach the gospel but also marks the center of Luke's concentric approach to teaching about this experience.

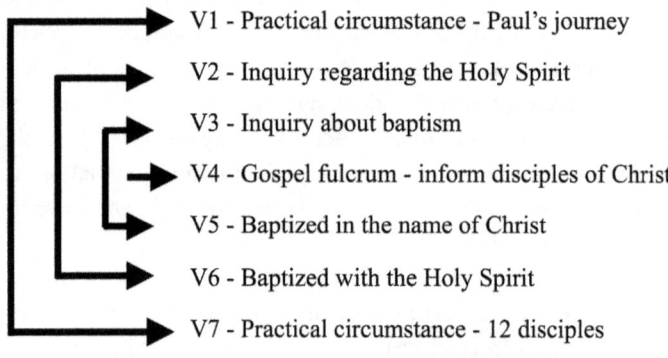

Concentric Construction of Luke 19:1–7

The fulcrum that Paul uses to correctly align the understanding of the inquisitive disciples is that of the good news of Jesus Christ and John's role as forerunner to the Messiah (Luke 3:1–18). John the Baptist engaged his audience with offensive statements, yet he created curiosity in their minds, which then brought about their own questions of how to respond to his message, "What should we do?" (Luke 3:10, 12, 14).[118] John then makes it

---

117. Hesselgrave and Rommen, *Contextualization: Meanings, Methods, and Models*, 98.

118. Malina, *New Testament World*, 154.

clear through his own understanding that the Messiah will follow him and that, by comparison, his baptism will be one of purification and completion.

The concentric constructions of Acts 19:1–7 have a center in verse 4, which is then surrounded by chiastic, parallel pairs of verses.[119] Verse 5 records the response of the people to the question posed in verse 3 regarding baptism. Verse 6 shows the baptism in the Holy Spirit, which fulfills their ignorance found in verse 2. Verse 7 finishes with a practical circumstance, where the disciples are presented as different because of the sending of Paul in verse 1 and his embodiment of *missio Dei* as an apostle.

The structure of this passage as written by Luke reveals the animating center of the gospel of Jesus Christ to Paul's evangelistic efforts. The gospel aligns, challenges, and brings about change to hearts for those who inquisitive and open to Christ. In another instance, Luke connects the experience of "hearts burning" with the opening of Scriptures, as in the case of the two disciples on the road to Emmaus (Luke 24:32). In short, people engaged by apostles/messengers with the information of the gospel look for an appropriate response. Further, the apostle/messenger, in this case Paul, desires to make disciples who will be of similar caliber in terms of service. The baptism in the Holy Spirit, as presented by Luke in Acts 19:1–7, is separate and subsequent to a salvific response.

CONCLUSION

What concludes this study of Lukan literature is the realization that the Holy Spirit inspires people to be sent, to proclaim, to gather, and to develop followers of Jesus Christ. The inspiration of the Spirit led to explicit actions which birthed a church charged with cross-cultural mission. The Disciple/Church Multiplication Cycle orders and characterizes the multiplication of faith communities by the guidance and empowerment of the Holy Spirit. How Luke narrates the work of Jesus, Paul, and others must be pragmatically considered while consistent openness to the Spirit is fostered.[120] Luke chose to include these passages that speak of the Holy Spirit interacting with humankind, so Theophilus would trust that he can assist in the efforts to share the gospel as well. Truly, the gospel will be preached *panta ta ethne*.

---

119. Maynet, *Rhetorical Argumentation in Biblical Texts*, 200.ed. A. Eriksson, T.H. Olbricht, and W. Übelacker (London: Bloomsbury, 2002

120. Allen, *Spontaneous Expansion of the Church*, loc. 26.

3

Sociocultural Factors Affecting General Swedish Perception of Pneumatological Activity

INTRODUCTION

Throughout its history as a country, Sweden exhibits a growing number of perspectives regarding spirituality. Where homogenous thought reigned up to 1000 CE because of communal survival, the following millennium found increased opportunities to embrace rational, secular values and artistic, individual expression. A *mångfald* (diversity) of perspectives regarding pneumatological activity developed alongside the government and Christianization of Sweden. The most prevalent perspective is that of Swedish secular humanism, which affects the perception of Swedes, influencing them to trust experience over unseen deity. The purpose of this section is to analyze the history and culture to understand factors that affect Swedish society's view of pneumatological activity.

HISTORICAL CULTURAL FACTORS CONTRIBUTING TO SWEDISH PERCEPTION OF PNEUMATOLOGICAL ACTIVITY

Studying the anthropological and sociological development of Swedish culture provides insight for better understanding the Swedish perception of pneumatological activity. The historical development of the governmental structure—from rural kings to an established monarchy to parliament—occurred at the same time as the Christian evangelization of Sweden. An analysis of government and religious activity in Sweden further uncovers Swedish perspective of the activity of the Holy Spirit.

From Paganism to Catholicism

Explorations of the Viking Age (800–1050 CE) allowed the Swedish Vikings to raid and encounter new cultures. Reciprocally, this new age of travel also allowed a missionary named Ansgar to venture into Sweden from 830 to 850. During this time, he encountered a people famous for their filthy and discourteous behavior.[1] Already a group to themselves, the Swedish Vikings received the gospel, which they challenged with their deeply engrained coarse behavior. After Ansgar's influence, the Christian faith was planted, grew, and began to be questioned during the next three hundred years by the Swedish people.[2] As a result of missionary work, the Swedish Catholic Church gathered and established itself in 1164. The founding of the church signaled the end of the worship of the Norse gods: Odin, Thor, and Frej. Across all Sweden, people would convert towards a faith in Jesus Christ.

From the 1200s to the 1300s, the church founded monasteries and convents, growing as part of the organizational structure of Sweden until it possessed one-fifth of the country's land, wealth, and political power. Simultaneously with this occurrence, regional kings fought and killed one another to gain control of the entire nation. The people's trust in government remained in continual flux as kings usurped one another, yet their trust in the church remained consistent as leadership was steadily directed from Rome. Through the consolidation of the monarchy, the proximity of the church presented opportunities for the church to serve the people and king of Sweden. In 1454, the church began to contribute part of its income to the central government, which mediated a financial role in the Swedish

---

1. Rynkiewich, *Soul, Self, and Society*, loc. 746.
2. Weibull, *Swedish History in Outline*, 16.

nation. A reliance upon government in place of the church would challenge how Swedes believed in supernatural activity.

Reformation of Church and State

The church would gradually become subject to the Swedish crown, rather than existing as an independent force. Swedish landowners would now own most of the land that had once belonged to regional kings. Once these kings died or were defeated in battle, a need for stability developed. A single throne and eventually a parliament that assumed decision-making responsibilities relieved this stress.[3] The central throne of King Gustav Vasa became the *Tingsrätt*, or Court of Decision, thereby holding the power of the land. It should be noted that Vasa held little interest in theological ideals, yet he was knowledgeable of their power over people.[4]

During shifts of political power between the invading Danish leadership and the Swedish king, Gustav Vasa, Martin Luther facilitated a reform movement on how the church was to function in relation to God and people. At this time, Vasa decided to remove support from the Roman Catholic Church, then transitioning influence towards the Lutheran Church. This action would establish the sovereignty of the state over the church while continuing to work in tandem. Thus, the country of Sweden was set on a course that would impact the country for centuries to come.

Developing Atheism

Western thought regards Friedrich Nietzsche (1844–1900) as the patron saint and forbearer of postmodern philosophy.[5] His academic career at the University of Basel in Germany earned him a professorship and chair of the department of philology at age twenty-five.[6] His negation of truth threatened modern thought.[7] Further, he believed that the ideal of a "true world" was not achievable by humankind. Nietzsche purported that the interpretation of life and the experience between subject and object exists only as an illusion.[8] His nihilistic stance prevented the very concept of a future to be

---

3. Witoszek and Trägårdh, *Culture and Crisis*, 37.
4. Kent, *The Soul of the North*, 20.
5. Grenz, *Primer on Postmodernism*, 16.
6. Hunter, *To Change the World*, loc. 6060.
7. Clark and Pippin, *Nietzsche on Truth and Philosophy*, 191.
8. Grenz, *Primer on Postmodernism*, 93.

of importance. Following his death, Nietzsche's sister, Elizabeth, published his writings across Europe. In the early 1900s, Ernest Thiel, a wealthy Swedish banker, translated Nietzsche's works into Swedish, as they helped him find freedom "from the taboos of Swedish society."[9] For an entire century, Nietzsche has contributed to the shift in Swedish philosophy from trust in God to an elevation of the self, removing any need to recognize God's pneumatological activity.

People's Home: *Folkhemmet*

Near the time of the introduction of Nietzschean thought to the Swedish people, the Swedish concept of government and healthcare centralization, the *Folkhemmet*, or the People's Home, would come to pass. The inner workings of centralized government can be summarized as an agreement between capitalism and socialism in which all people within Sweden contribute to the collective care for all. In 1860, the medical system changed hands from the Swedish State Church to the Swedish government in the establishment of the *Folkhem*. The advent of *Folkhemmet* would create an updated, internally consistent system of healthcare for all Swedes, based on the *Folkhem*. The formation of the People's Home in 1932 was a major event that further contributed to the removal of the church's influence on the municipal life of Sweden. This contributes to the cultural perception of God's divine work, which would hold an "irresistible attraction" to Swedes.[10] *Folkhemmet* provided a social contract in which an individual could belong to a collective, in this case the country of Sweden, and maintain ownership of material things while contributing to the commonwealth.[11] Obligation to self and the greater Swedish community would assume the position of the most important ideology in the land.[12]

The Nominalization of the Lutheran Church

Between 1525 and 1593, the Lutheran Church would fend off Roman Catholic resurgences, taking its place as the chosen faith of the realm. Changing from the model of the Catholic Church, where only the priests read the Bible during Mass, the Reformation encouraged the Swedish people to read

9. Hunter, *To Change the World*, loc. 6068.
10. Rojas, *Sweden after the Swedish Model*, 7.
11. Rousseau, *Social Contract* (1920.
12. Trägårdh, interview.

Scripture in the Swedish language and in the privacy of their own homes. Distrust of the Roman Catholic Church lingered, however, casting increased suspicion towards the newly formed Swedish (Lutheran) Church.[13]

Over the centuries, the waning belief in God occurred as Swedes turned towards social systems for their well-being.[14] In the year 2000, the state and church split. The church became a separate entity cut loose from federal funding and holding no power in parliamentary process. As a result of the separation, the Lutheran Church experienced the "Great Escape." One million people left the church, choosing to keep their money instead of diverting a percentage of their tax dollars to the church.[15] In 2011, it was reported that only 15 percent of the membership of the Swedish Lutheran Church believed that Jesus Christ existed at all.[16] From this same study, it was found that the same percentage of the church are confessing atheists. The primary role of the Swedish Lutheran Church evolved from being a facilitator of worship to a facilitator of Swedish tradition.[17]

Effects of Postmodernity

Postmoderns reject given solutions and create their own answers. Where truth once was preached from the Bible, new books and faiths have introduced other pathways for spirituality. Within one thousand years, the pendulum of faith has swung from pagan gods and human sacrifice, through Catholicism and Lutheranism, to atheism and the present postmodernity.[18] The Swedish culture displays a growing distrust of the church and of pyramidal power structures in general. Since the separation of church and state, Swedes continue to place their faith primarily in themselves.

Contemporary Swedish Postmodernism

Preceding the 1900s, a pre-postmodern influence resulted from the general disintegration of what was culturally accepted as truth.[19] This process of secularization eroded the Swedish people's trust in Christianity. A notable

---

13. Grenz, *Primer on Postmodernism*, 84.
14. Gibbs, *In Name Only*, 166.
15. Svenska Kyrkan, *Inträden I och Utträden*.
16. Landes, "Swedish Church Members 'Don't Believe in Jesus.'"
17. Wiman, "Kyrkan Är Fortfarande Vårt Största Kulturhus."
18. Piper et al, *Supremacy of Christ*, 40.
19. Hunter, *To Change the World*, 207.

Swedish cultural anthropologist finds that post-Christian Sweden has largely retained the ceremonies of faith yet removed God.[20] The center of worship within the Swedish Lutheran Church, once being Jesus Christ, was now supplanted by devotion to humanism.[21]

Summary

The intertwined historical threads of government and religion reveal motifs of secularization, distrust of the church, and a general faith in the Swedish government. The socialization of Sweden held much influence alongside the Christian evangelization of Sweden, affecting how Swedes would eventually regard the church. Swedes learned to trust the government in place of the church, a result of government and church changes, the assimilation of atheism and postmodern thought, as well as reliance upon the *Folkhemmet* model. Historical Swedish perception affected an increased reliance upon government and the adoption of postmodernity. The resulting perception of pneumatological activity based on these influences is one of indifference to the spiritual potency of Christianity and a recognition of the prominence of Christianity as history. Contemporary cultural factors further an inherited disregard for pneumatological activity.

CONTEMPORARY CULTURAL FACTORS CONTRIBUTING TO SWEDISH PERCEPTION OF PNEUMATOLOGICAL ACTIVITY

Present Swedish mentality is a culmination of centuries of development. The Swedish Lutheran Church is known as a warehouse of Swedish history. In conjunction with other cultural clues, focused research of Swedish thoughts on religion can enhance efforts to understand how they perceive pneumatological activity in contemporary Sweden.

Hermeneutic of Secular Humanism

Secular humanism must be understood as a construct of values that makes sense to those who subscribe to them. Examination of the sociological grouping of Swedish people provides key insights into their perspective of

---

20. Trägårdh, interview.
21. Gibbs, *In Name Only*, 170.

pneumatological activity. Shared attitudes and perspectives toward an object or person provide the basis for a people's choice of grouping in the Western setting of Sweden.[22] Though other groups may critique the actions of a secular humanist, the social aim of the group remains intact, strengthened through their relationships to others of like mind. Their affinity towards a common ideology can result in a heightened influence within the group, underpinning the commitment of the participants.[23, 24] Feedback which a secular humanist receives from their actions directly benefits their trust in constructs of tangible human accomplishment in place of intangible divine interaction.

Secular Humanism Defined

A strong representative grouping of secular humanist professionals who share similar ideals can be found in the international Council of Secular Humanism.[25] They define secular humanism as a construct of life that does not acknowledge a deity, while considering their ideologies as distinct from atheism. A hallmark of their organization centers on their proposal that the affective dimension of a person exists to itself without help.[26] Further, reliance upon empirical and rational thought rooted in the present, while also relying upon the philosophical and academic endeavors of past thinkers, characterizes social groupings of secular humanists.[27] As an extension of the diversity within secular humanism, the social contract of Sweden generously allows for individual expression of oneself in keeping with the trust in the *Folkhemmet*.

While rationality and empiricism remain, traits claimed by Swedish secular humanists, those who subscribe to a life built on secular humanism lack an epicenter to their code of living.[28] They limit their beliefs to the tangible world, trusting solely on the ability of humanity to rely on its own intelligence and rational flavor of morality.

---

22. Erikson and Erikson, *Life Cycle Completed*, 18.
23. Halldorf, *Pentecostal Politics in a Secular World*, 5–6.
24. Kraus, "Research Paradigms and Meaning Making," 761.
25. Council for Secular Humanism, "Secular Humanist Declaration."
26. Flynn, "Secular Humanism Defined."
27. Weigel, *Cube and the Cathedral*, 49.
28. Taylor, *Secular Age*, loc. 163.

Swedish Secular Humanism Defined

A secondary group, *Humanisterna*, provides a reference point for defining Swedish secular humanism (SSH). *Humanisterna* exists as a non-profit association of Swedish people who have formed an interest group recognized by the Swedish government. As is the process for all non-profit organizations, the banking system approves their *stadgar* (statutes), ensuring they have a shared interest in an ideology, object, or person.[29] The confirmation of both government and the financial sector gives weight to Swedish-based interest groups. Most churches, clubs, athletic teams, and social activities participate in this formalized process for establishing organizations. These groups are structured to include self-government, money handling, and reporting annual goals. These aspects lend stability to each organization.

The organizational structure of *Humanisterna* ensures that the group has a voice in egalitarian Sweden.[30] This group, however, is representative of a normal occurrence in Sweden, that of people who will be referred to as Swedish secular humanists or SSH. Although Sweden has separated the church from the state in both formation and influence, the SSH remains committed to removing religious influence from the world altogether. They believe that a populous void of spiritual influence would answer questions of ethics and politics in a more reasonable manner.[31] As a non-profit, they have decided that the best outcomes in life originate from the secular perspective. Further, they do not consider religion as having any positive aspects and bolster their support of secular relief organizations with comparisons to the dishonorable financial mishandlings of the Swedish State Church.[32]

Swedish Secular Humanism Preunderstanding

In direct contrast to the Christian hermeneut who interprets Scripture within a faith community, an SSH adopts a particular set of precepts with which to interpret humanity to humans.[33] To an SSH, humanity already contains the truth that it needs to propel the world forward in development. They do not recognize any spiritual source as influential to their direction. By definition, this understanding aligns their group to the greater European

---

29. RPTM, "Stadgar—Ideella Föreningar."
30. Rojas, *Beyond the Welfare State*, 19.
31. Humanisterna, "Idéprogram."
32. Sturmark, "Lämna Svenska."
33. Lewis, *Missiological Research*, loc. 1620.

problem of secularization.[34] This affective dimension of the SSH makes them attractive amongst other strains of ideology within Sweden.

Truth

For an SSH, truth exists as the ideal found within one's realization of freedom from religious influence.[35] They believe that the source of this liberating truth comes not from a deity but from within oneself. Secularism, by definition, simply substitutes God with oneself as a central locus of worship. Despite this trend, rituals and traditions continue within church settings where secularization is evident. In a postmodern climate, truth becomes relative to the human and to their own viewpoint, supported by critical realism.[36] The truth, according to *Humanisterna*, exists within human potential yet allows the disjunction of postmodernity. This ideological freedom thwarts forward motion within humanist organizations, splintering the focused goal of SSHs into an array of self-centered activity.

Revelation

As the global church, Christians hope in the equality and unity found in Christ (Rom 8:16–17).[37] In contrast, SSH's hope for equality and unity is found in the future of humanity's invention and interdependence. The method in which to evangelize, however, differs in how each ideology carries out its message to humanity. Christians profess empowerment drawn from God's love for people. As bearers of God's love, they act as change agents through servanthood, finding humble strength in their kerygmatic task (Phil 2; John 3:16).[38] Conversely, humanists choose their primary means for revealing truth through opposing religious entities. Through opposition, an SSH believes that they give others the cognitive and affective room to grow into their potential.[39] This opposition supplies independence from faith in the teachings of the church, allowing individuals to affix their eyes upon a more natural goal, as opposed to supernatural aspiration.

---

34. Weigel, *Cube and the Cathedral*, 51.
35. Humanisterna, "Idéprogram."
36. Grenz, *Primer on Postmodernism*, 89.
37. Catholic/universal.
38. Rogers and Steinfatt, *Intercultural Communication*, 40.
39. Weigel, *Cube and the Cathedral*, 54.

Future

The SSH possesses an alternative eschatological hope, one that finds confidence in the present age through humans caring for humans, which is reflected in the Swedish Lutheran Church's relief and development programs, of which they themselves may retain nominal membership.[40] Influenced by humans, psychologists and scientists document the past through numerical evaluation while charting industrial and medical successes. Technological advances would not be their only evidence to defend their doctrine yet would be a primary factor in the recent globalized trend of these virtual sociological groupings. The SSH's future would be found in their kin, who would carry on the beliefs of their parents. As the secularization process continues through familial lineage, the heritage, rituals, and traditions of an SSH strengthen.[41] The SSH trusts in humanity and has no reason to look beyond their interdependent relationships. Also, they restrict their non-formal covenant to those who exclusively believe and trust with a similar perspective.[42] For their future to result in equality and unity, the SSH utilizes opposition to any religious organization in the belief that secular humanists will reveal truth in the process.

Functional Relationships

In establishing a societal environment where acculturation can occur, social relationships outside of familiar SSH circles remains necessary. As SSHs view humanity as the source of revealed truth for the future, they seek to assist others in recognizing their hermeneutic and communication as appropriate in reaching goals that an SSH would value.[43] The SSH relies upon a preunderstanding which values egalitarian thought, unified focus, and the cognition of those engaged in conversation to build an argument through reason.[44] As a result, examining SSH's interaction with other humans benefits this study. Human-to-human and human-deity interaction also remain germane to this research.[45]

---

40. Svenska Kyrkan, "Vårt Arbete."
41. Grunlan and Mayers, *Cultural Anthropology*, 168.
42. Hall, *Dance of Life*, 86–90.
43. Jonker, *Global Hermeneutics?*, 47.ed. Knut Holter and Louis.C. Jonker, International Organization for the Study of the Old Testament (Atlanta, GA: Society of Biblical Literature, 2010
44. Lingenfelter, *Transforming Culture*, 26.
45. Bevans, *Models of Contextual Theology*, 55.

Towards Humanity

Understanding the Swedish context helps to explain the interaction and communication between an SSH and another human.[46] As the SSH values care given to other humans, recent developments in Sweden provide a revealing backdrop for understanding how others perceive SSH values.[47] Known as a homogenous country alongside Norway, Swedes score high in secular-rational values and in self-expression.[48] Within the homogeneity of Swedish culture, the effect of postmodernity affords any self-expression to each individual Swede. As a result, Swedes identify with what the Swedish social contract dictates as well as what the individual thinks is right and true. When combining this mentality with immigrants who value tradition and physical survival, societal challenges arise.

Throughout the twentieth century and into the twenty-first, Sweden has opened its doors to refugees and immigrants seeking safety and jobs. Most of the migrant movement occurred within the past one hundred years, which provides recent experiences to view the process of assimilation.[49] Sweden is one of the few countries of Europe that has welcomed refugees of the current refugee crisis, which began in 2015.[50] This welcome was short-lived, however, given a resurgence of in-group out-group bias towards refugees.[51] This has resulted in a conflicted message sent by Sweden of both hospitality and dismissal.

In welcoming refugees to Sweden, a tension has grown between the indifference and rationality of humanism, which relies upon the government for refugee relief, clashing with that of forgiveness, hope, and proximity as found in the Christian Church, which relies upon its members to exemplify Christ's care for others. Swedish culture showcases this tension in the political reception of refugees. A systems approach to causality in understanding the actions and reactions of the SSH provides an integrated perspective on present-day interaction with globalized culture.[52]

---

46. Shaw and van Engen, *Communicating God's Word*, 110.
47. Alcala, "Humanisterna Tiger Om Grunden För Sin Tro."
48. World Values Survey, "WVS Database."
49. Migrationsverket, "Migration—Statistics."
50. Ahlstrand, "Många Flyktingar Söker."
51. Johansson, "Sd-Nej Till Flyktingar."
52. Hiebert, *Transforming Worldviews*, loc. 1572.

Equality

The egalitarian nature of the SSH influences human interaction in the country.[53] Language illustrates this societal symmetry within the person-to-person dyad.[54] For example, one finds students addressing their teachers by their first names. In addition, a new pronoun, *hen*, has diminished the usage of *han* (he) and *hon* (she) while simultaneously trying to retain personal identity as a human being aside from gender attribution. Although primarily used in print media, the new term indicates the inclusive yet nebulous center of Swedish communication.[55] The SSH's perspective on equality appears within their intrinsic value of inclusion, which visibly manifests *mångfald* (diversity). This diversity remains acceptable to the country so long as all agree to the Swedish social contract. This tolerance, then, for diversity and difference within the populous of Sweden is maintained and allowed within a mindset that must remain grounded in democracy.[56] Evidence for equality comes from equal representation of each voice within Sweden.

Unity

Sweden formed a relationship with Germany during WWII to trade iron, wood, and coal. They also allowed safe passage of German forces between Norway and Finland between 1939 and 1940, which escalated global attention to their perceived neutral position.[57] This interaction between the Swedish and German governments revealed the unity and allegiance that Swedes held within their worldview.[58] The totalitarian rule of Nazism, although it tried, could not establish its government within the secular environment of Sweden because of the homogeny of the host culture. German atheistic humanism could not relate to the Swedish secular humanism which characterized the country. While not patriotic, Swedish allegiance to the underlying ideal of democracy means that Swedes not only value equality but also unity in relation to this ideal.[59] Resisting the close connection with Nazi Germany while enjoying their business, Sweden emerged from the global

---

53. Hofstede et al., *Cultures and Organizations*, Loc 1149.
54. Grunlan and Mayers, *Cultural Anthropology*, 89.
55. Neuman, "He, She or Hen?."
56. Trägårdh, interview.
57. Witoszek and Trägårdh, *Culture and Crisis*, 133.
58. Trägårdh, interview.
59. Löfgren, "Why Most Swedes Don't Care about National Day."

conflict maintaining a "Swedish" diplomacy and economy. Clearly, Sweden and Germany hosted differing strains of humanism.

Unity appears not only in the past struggles of wartime but also in the affective dimension of care in today's Sweden. Caring for fellow humans remains incredibly important to an SSH. It is noteworthy that membership within a voluntary organization in Sweden requires a high commitment to the shared philosophy, which is telling of SSHs.[60] The SSH values unity in cognitive and affective relationships; cognitive thought strengthening internal connection and affective values produces external outreach. Both Protestant members of churches and secular humanists share the transcendent value of care.[61]

Terrorist attacks in Sweden have caused disarray in society, yet unification followed soon after. In 2010, a suicide bomber took his own life and injured two bystanders in downtown Stockholm.[62] In April of 2017, an Uzbekistani man hijacked a delivery truck and plowed through a crowded pedestrian street, killing four people attempting to flee.[63] Once, a search began to find the man who had hijacked the truck. Traditionally, Sweden had been slow to reveal the suspect to media, yet within twenty-four hours authorities released the name and nationality of the man in question.[64] Further, vigils to encourage the community, combined with a collective confirmation of the police force's response, revealed their national trust and strength in being Swedish.[65]

In a society known for humility because of the deeply engrained *jantelagen*[66] of the culture, public displays of pride following the tragic events could not have been forecast.[67] As leading Swedish anthropologists criticize the rhetoric of Sweden's mass media, the public display of community coupled with the declaration by Stefan Löfven reveals a unified Sweden in his statement, "Our message will always be clear: You cannot suppress us.

---

60. Trägårdh, *Society in Northern Europe*, 97.
61. Trägårdh, *Society in Northern Europe*, 96.
62. Anderson and Anderson, "Stockholm Hit by Blasts after Threatening Message."
63. Christys, et al., "Sweden Terror."
64. By, "Ensamvarg."
65. Bergstedt, "Terrorattacken"; Said-Moorhouse and Jones, "Stockholm Unites after Attack."
66. The idea of *Jantelagen* (*-lagen*) is described by Norwegian author Aksel Sandemose, who wrote of a town called Jante. In *A Fugitive Crosses His Tracks*, he describes ten laws that describe the group behavior of Scandinavians. In essence, no one is special across the backdrop of egalitarian small-town life as everyone knows everyone else's past and present works.
67. Bromgard et al., „Janteloven"; Hofstede, „Sweden."

You cannot control our lives. You will never win."[68] This spoken address further grounded the secular humanistic perspective of the Swedish people given the rhetoric Löfven chose to communicate.[69]

Opposition

The heart of an SSH seeks to drive out religious influences upon the governing processes of society.[70] Their collective voice opposes the institutional teachings of the Swedish Lutheran Church, yet approves areas of affinity found in the biblical text, e.g., love, hope, unity, etc.[71] Secular humanism finds no better representation in the governmental system[72] than through the concept formed in 1860 known as the *Folkhem*.[73] A series of ideals establishing the *Folkhem* removed medical care from Swedish churches and transferred this power to the upper echelons of governance, building the reliance of the Swedish people upon the progressive centralization of their democracy. This progression of consolidation would also run parallel to a concurrent process of secularization throughout the country.[74]

Within the construct of the *Folkhem*, opportunity for debate naturally arose within the purportedly equal and unified body.[75] The egalitarian governing table allowed voices who understood the social games of the Swedish people to oppose one another. The autonomous Swedish citizen who has one's affairs in order in terms of wealth, taxes, and civil duty may participate.[76] Internal debate within the government would strengthen the country; critiquing ideals helps reveal truth and enable Swedes to envision the future in unity. Both Christians and secular humanists may participate in society as equals, with political elections deciding the validity of their debates. Further, whether one is religious or not, all are tested by the process of opposition.[77]

---

68. Regeringen och Regeringskansliet, "Statement by Prime Minister Stefan Löfven"; Trägårdh, interview.
69. Ong and Hartley, *Orality and Literacy*, 75.
70. Humanisterna, "Idéprogram."
71. Witoszek and Trägårdh, *Culture and Crisis*, 134.
72. Rojas, *Sweden after the Swedish Model*, 7.
73. As a tool for identifying and differing between the developments of these ideologies, *Folkhem* is a precursor to *Folkhemmet*.
74. Survey, "WVS Database."
75. Grenz, *Primer on Postmodernism*, 121.
76. Trägårdh, interview.
77. Engeli et al., *Morality Politics in Western Europe*, 7; Uggla, *Ricoeur, Hermeneutics,*

The currents of morality that underlie the differing perspectives within the government all participate in the process of opposition, usually as a last resort of differentiation between worldviews.[78] Morality rarely finds media attention within the arena of government, yet policy and law within the secular environment demand adherence. When those of the Free Churches propose laws and changes, the Swedish secular humanists remain ready to represent the homogenous population of Sweden to oppose their proposals.[79]

As time progresses, the realization that people remain as humanity's only hope appears in no higher forum than the Swedish parliament, which increasingly values Swedish identity over an identity found in Christianity or any variety of religion. The opinion-building endeavors of debate are met, however, by the fractalization of opinion, even within the realm of the SSH. The plurality of worldviews contained in the homogenous mixture of Sweden seems to neutralize and nominalize any form of fundamentalism, be it Christian, Muslim, or any other affiliation.[80]

Towards Deity

The SSH recognizes the existence of religious beliefs in Sweden's population yet considers these systems of faith draconian to government and society. To an SSH, the negation of a deity from the tangible existence of humanity provides freedom and release from constraint as they ground knowledge in the natural, providing a shared human destiny.[81] By freeing oneself from the influence of a sacred text, culture and humanity can affirm the present iteration and scientific inventions of the populous.[82] Just as the church provides the greatest storehouse of past cultural history, present culture offers the greatest storehouse of values that matter most to an SSH.[83] Since the greater populous does not identify as professing Christians but more as cultural Christians, they illustrate a version of Christianity that remains deeply affected by secularity for the sake of pursuing earthly endeavors.[84] The influence of a sacred text is not primary in the series of lenses considered

---

and Globalization, 82.

78. Engeli et al., *Morality Politics in Western Europe*, 14.
79. Halldorf et al., *Between the State and the Eucharist*, 9.
80. Niebuhr, *Christ and Culture*, xlix.
81. Loder, *Logic of the Spirit*, 72.
82. Witoszek and Trägårdh, *Culture and Crisis*, 134.
83. Wiman, "Vårt Största Kulturhus."
84. Ottestig, "Vill Inte Att Kristna Ska Kalla Sig Kristna.."

by the SSH. An increased distance in physical and social proximity from a sacred text results in a higher probability that a culture will experience a secularization process that looks to themselves for cognitive and affective sustenance, much like the Epicureans and Stoics of Paul's Athenian experience (Acts 17).

Tolerance

In postmodern Sweden, where meaning and reverence remain relatively detached from historically sacred sources of knowledge and illumination, interpretations of life are equally respected and allowed to grow alongside each other.[85] In certain expressions of Swedish culture, the prevalence of SSH thought as a thematic backdrop for functional relationships forces a subtle non-recognition of any divine being to participate in society. To an SSH, God is dead. Reworded to reflect their understanding: there is no God. Admitting to the fluency of semiology in an American-European culture that prides itself on proficiency and efficiency of financial transaction and cultural assimilation, the simple removal of a cross from a place of worship makes the building more acceptable to the larger populous.[86]

Equality in diversity exists, yet Swedish intolerance of these organizations can lead to a removal of that which they perceive to be unwelcoming to non-adherents within the Swedish context. The formation of the aforementioned non-profit organization structure of Sweden attempts to ensure that all Swedes have access to each and every affinity group within the culture.[87] Sacred texts are considered intolerant, which then causes the SSH to remove the sacred text's influence over Swedish society. Sweden holds to controlled pluralism, allowing belief within the people with a presiding government based in humanism. Not only does secular humanism color the perspectives of the people of Sweden as a whole, but it sequesters the practices of ritual belief from public influence.

Unity as Defined by an SSH

A pluralistic perspective and syncretistic practice occupy the space left by the removal of God in Sweden. In the past, scholars labeled secularization a social myth, but the sociological implication of mass movement of

---

85. Cowdell, *Is Jesus Unique?*, 263.
86. Hall, *Dance of Life*, 32; Ong and Hartley, *Orality and Literacy*, 75.
87. RPTM, "Stadgar—Ideella Föreningar."

people away from church membership has dispelled this idea, qualifying the concept as reality.[88] The secularization of the adherents of the Swedish Lutheran Church introduces other religious-based ideologies blurring the lines of Christian moral boundaries. Equal representation of all faiths is welcomed in the Swedish Lutheran Church, which allows equal influence from not only biblical Scripture but other sacred texts as well. For example, the introduction of Mother Earth to Swedes within the Swedish Lutheran Church in Linköping allows one to critically realize themselves as a part of naturalized divinity in relationship to earth. The deconversion of Swedes towards secular humanism inevitably affects the trajectory of Swedish politics and how their society functions.

Unity exists in the groupings of adherents to SSH ideals.[89] Through their shared efforts, they give to care organizations. Volunteer organizations, however, suffer because of the strong centralized government and the services that are already provided to the Swedish people.[90] Reliance on the government as the main caregiver and influencer of Sweden provides a general sense of security for the SSH.

Opposition as a Tool for the SSH

The non-profit organizations of Swedish secular humanism are built upon volunteers who pay a fee for membership, enabling them to share in the benefits surrounding their common ideology. This group shares the same classification as Swedes who gather around tennis, chess, Christ, and politics. Not unlike a religious non-profit, the SSH group retains a governmental status alongside sport-based associations.[91] This rallying point differs from a schedule of game matches or craft meetings. An SSH's involvement in lobbying at parliament is substantial in their internal reports.[92] Their stance in achieving "critical mass" in "being an evident, opposing force" in politics provides a view into how they define success. They celebrate opposition to the deity and to the deified, particularly when policy follows their lead. No matter the rhetoric they may choose to use towards religious groups, their rights as a non-profit within Sweden ensures that their voice can be shared.

Perpetuating their opposition to religious function in society, *Humanisterna* has published claims that religion in Christ provided the

88. Glasner, *Sociology of Secularisation*, 20.
89. Humanisterna, "Idéprogram."
90. Trägårdh, *Society in Northern Europe*, 176.
91. Trägårdh, *Society in Northern Europe*, 180.
92. Alcala, "Humanisterna Tiger Om Grunden För Sin Tro."

basis for Nazism.[93] Collusion between humanists and Nazis during WWII reveals how closely they related to each other, and the church stood apart from their partnership.[94] When the relationship to Germany ended after WWII, the Nazi nationalistic influence propelled forward a Swedish plan of humanism in existence since the 1920s. SSHs employed eugenics, the engineering of biological succession, to sterilize their own people who exhibited birth defects and other undesirable traits.[95] Their decided stance in opposition to God demands that humanists fight any ideology that subscribes to a deity or threatens the forward movement of humanism. The assimilation of undesirable people into the Swedish *Folkhemmet* posed a threat to Swedish purity, which proved problematic. In relationship to both humanity and to deity, SSHs oppose heterogeneity, which is not defined by their stringent scientific standards. Further, opposition of religion has been held akin to opposition of any ideology that is not a strain of Swedish secular humanism. The SSH trusts in a tangibly present humanity as the future of the country.

Summary

Swedish secular humanism does not currently realize how a divine being or force could interact with people to the point of constructing a favorable environment for humans to exist. Their idea of fairness and care remains rooted in their own efforts and understanding. Material success limits religious influence within a secularized society like Sweden. No matter the reaction of the church, the bolstered ideology of an SSH is well-established in Sweden as holding high influence over the culture and may affect the interpretation of any manifested spiritual phenomena occurring within the church.

SWEDISH ACTIONS BASED ON THEIR PERCEPTION OF PNEUMATOLOGICAL ACTIVITY

Historically, Swedish society has defined the voice of the present iteration of the Christian Church. The egalitarian society allows the church to exist alongside the myriad other social, non-profit organizations. The secularization of Sweden provides fertile soil for a pluralistic expression of the church, yet

---

93. Alcala, "Humanisterna Tiger Om Grunden För Sin Tro."
94. Yoder, *Politics of Jesus*, 145.
95. Ratzka, "Eradication Of 'Deviants'."

it does not allow for a supernatural God to intervene in the world today. An SSH does not recognize the church as God's instrument of salvation for the world and condemns any thought that may separate Christians as special in comparison to all other Swedes. This is *jantelagen* at work.

Pluralism

Despite the increasing attributes of secularity and the country's status as "one of the least religious countries in the world," Swedish individuals allow and partake in selected spiritual experiences.[96] Per their cultural preferences for communication, however, they allow time for coffee, conversation, and sharing rationally founded viewpoints, regardless of agreement.[97] At the same time, the generous latitude for religious tolerance found within this egalitarian perspective typically results in apathy and indifference to any form of religious practice.[98]

This indifference has led to a new spiritual frontier, one in which an SSH's designation remains culturally approved, where anything goes. The SSH may view all faiths as having pneumatological activity: Buddhists may meditate into a trance; Muslims pray in unison and direction; and Christians reflect on the grace afforded themselves through Christ. The SSH will simply regard these activities as rituals of peace that bring rest to one's body. While the Christian finds that communion with God helps them in supernaturally transcending their circumstances, the SSH will view this as just one of many ritual occurrences that function in similar ways.

Allowance in Swedish Culture

Pluralism allows all expressions of faith to be perceived as equal in intent, praxis, and eschatology. Swedish pluralism expresses itself sociologically in group interests ranging from Qigong yoga in the Swedish Lutheran churches to North American Indian meditative rituals employed to combat stress.[99] Within the limitless breadth of spiritual ambiguity, the typical Swede weaves a tapestry of pluralism, paying little attention to the universals that strict adherents within traditional faith structures would gather around, engaging in both the condemnation and creation of makeshift religions. Centuries of

---

96. Horton, *Acts*, 425.
97. York, *Missions in the Age of the Spirit*, 86.
98. Survey, "WVS Database"; WIN/Gallup, "End of Year Survey."
99. Hall, *Dance of Life*, 196.

an imperialized Catholic/Lutheran Church structure have given way to the rejection of the ecclesial in favor of the tangible, sacred, secular spaces for individual religious practice.[100] Secularism has not eradicated faith, but it has created a *mångfald* or diversity of utterances within the Swedish people. This outpouring can be found throughout the nation, especially in urban centers where university education occurs.

Within the social structure of Sweden, new opportunities exist for students who have proven themselves in *gymnasiet* (high school) and who have qualified for the university. The *mångfald* of organizations that greet those on the campuses of Sweden confirms the new freedom individuals now have from their families. Further, the freedom to do as one pleases at the university allows an escape from moral constraint.[101] Compounding this influence on these young adults is the idea that within the social contract of Sweden, there exists a presiding notion that only self-sufficient, autonomous individuals are allowed into group activities.[102] Thus, individuals who have formed their individual belief system can congregate to celebrate each separate facet of their spirituality. That a monotheism would occupy their heart space seems far too efficient. This cascade of Epicurean/Stoic spirituality within the egalitarian construct of Sweden creates a provisionally tolerant flavor of pluralism.

Effects of Pluralism on Existing Church Structure

The abandonment of the church in favor of a self-prescribed faith was substantiated in the exodus of one million members from the Swedish Lutheran Church between 2000 and 2010.[103] Indicators leading up to this mass attrition were evident in media, personal communication, and the political system. Swedish people's affinity for a socially sufficient nominality results in vast removal of membership in the Church of Sweden. It is entirely acceptable that a citizen engages in syncretistic religious practice while still venerating the empty church buildings scattered across the country as cultural and historical museums.[104]

---

100. Trägårdh, *Society in Northern Europe*, 206.
101. Svenska Kyrkan, "Historik.."
102. Ostwalt, *Secular Steeples*, 79.2012
103. Berggren and Trägårdh, Är Svensken Människa?, 48.
104. Alcala, "Humanisterna Tiger Om Grunden För Sin Tro."

Cultural Homogeneity

The group mentality of Sweden strongly holds to the concept of "we" as a social norm, while making substantial space for the "I."[105] Regarding the country's centralized government, the collective "we" expects better collective services with little bureaucracy, resulting in streamlined implicit communication within the organization. Swedes have no problem receiving and expediently returning a letter from the government requiring their signature, yet when a religious organization sends a letter requiring a signature for approval, they often view it with suspicion.[106]

Swedish homogeneity attenuates the diversity that Sweden boasts of to conform to the linguistic and social construct that its governmental system requires. Where all are individuals, the "we" must be emphasized for the sake of Swedish infrastructure. Within this logic, conformity to *Jämställdhet*, or equality in social standing, is necessary to give voice to the egalitarian voices within the international community. This is an ideal practice to share about Sweden in an economical sense, yet not all Swedes believe the same about religion, governance, and welfare. While this represents Sweden's acceptance of pluralism quite well, it does not override the influence of the SSH mentality.

Pluralism at Work in World Council of Churches 1968, Uppsala, Sweden

The fluid theoscape of Sweden has virtually silenced the potency of the church as a missional voice in society. A study written by two groups for the World Council of Churches (WCC) between 1962 and 1966 produced findings indicative of a missiology which would rather spectate about God's work rather than participate in it.[107] Coincidentally, these findings were presented at Uppsala, Sweden's WCC conference in 1968. The study called on the ecumenical fellowship to consider a God-world-church model in place of God-church-world. In light of this shift, the study reframed the trend of secularization as the "fruit of the gospel" and urged the church to abandon its "heretical structures" of mission and evangelization.[108]

Further, the study bore the influence of Johannes Hoekendijk, who likened the role of the church to the appendix of a book; the church exists

---

105. Wiman, "Vårt Största Kulturhus."
106. Wästberg, "New Melting Pot."
107. Hiebert, *Transforming Worldviews*, loc. 1790.
108. Hoekendijk, *Missionary Structures*.

solely for historical reference to God's works in the world.[109] Hoekendijk hoped that the decentralized church would be at work in the world in mission, positing that there would be an ideological conflict with the evangelical structures of mission.[110] While he did not emphasize evangelism as the focus of this mission, he did hope for justice to the poor and downtrodden of society, restoring God's pneumatological charge of the cosmos rather than sequestering his power to flow in and out of a christocentric church.[111]

Reversing the secularization of the group-oriented, individualized Swedish citizen can only come from the reidentification process of salvation. As each person is convinced internally of their right to a pluralistic faith, this same internal conviction of fullness found by the work of the Holy Spirit would need to be recognized by the individual.[112] To reach the individual Swede, a great disservice would occur should the modernized evangelical church form of "service" be qualified as the only legitimate iteration of the church in mission.[113] Jesus Christ modeled one-on-one, personal encounters in which he himself was the change agent. In time, however, this incarnation has been all but fully exchanged for the bolstering efforts of church centrism. Removing Jesus Christ as the center to either the church-centric evangelical service or to social-centric service per Hoekendijk provides similar results. Where there once was emphasis of congruency regarding dogma in the church, there would now be congruency with tradition for the humanist. Both are forms of faith structure without the need for a Savior. Nothing in the church pertains to God's active mission, according to Hoekendijk's studious prophecy. Following Jesus Christ as Lord is a narrow option within a pluralistic bandwidth, defined by one's latitude of worldview exposure and spiritual imagination. The Apostle Paul wrote to churches through a reflective and corrective attitude, yet unlike Hoekendijk, he included encouragement to follow closer to God while Hoekendijk merely cemented his description of the ineffectualness and apathy of the contemporary church.

Media

Sweden boasts a government-funded communications network consisting of radio, television, and internet provision for ten million people. As Swedish is the primary language of the country, society requires all inhabitants,

109. Alm, interview.
110. Hoedemaker, "Legacy of J. C. Hoekendijk," 168.
111. Arthur, "Missiology: Missio Dei."
112. Yates, *Christian Mission*, 197.
113. Arthur, "Missiology: Missio Dei"; Anderson, *Ministry on the Fireline*, 49.

including new immigrants, to be literate in Swedish to partake in social living. This comes as pressure from the government to do all that one can "to become employable."[114] By requiring participation in the culture of communication, Swedes uphold two of their highest values according to the implementation of the *Folkhemmet*: (1) to do right by oneself and (2) to do right by the *Jämställdhet* equality's standards.

Explicit actions which accompany the work of the Spirit—a transformed life, a healed person, the very existence of a vibrant church—may be understood as pneumatological activity in Sweden. By examining the media's handling of the visible activity of the Holy Spirit, one may see the foundational hermeneutic of a secular humanistic Sweden in action through the context of both secular and Christian media.

Perception of Church

The collective activity of the Holy Spirit can be found in the faith communities planted and thriving throughout Sweden. When a church functions as a traditional Pentecostal church that operates in the gifts of the Spirit, little to no attention is paid to it. This indicates that Hoekendijk's perspective persists in forecasting how Sweden treats pneumatological activity.

One continuing trend in Sweden, however, does bring Swedes into these Pentecostal churches. Weddings in these churches may provide an opening into the humanist's heart. Swedish couples typically opt to hold weddings in church buildings rather than outdoors. For a people who do not often attend church, they remain open to hearing about God and engaging in spiritual expression during these types of church rituals.[115] To non-Christian Swedes, the perception that God is supernaturally present creates a feeling that they must not lie, revealing a moral awareness. Indeed, participation in ritual holds implicit spiritual meaning to Swedes.

Still, *Pingst* churches struggle to reach society. This remains especially true considering a shooting incident in 2004 by a *Pingst* pastor in Knutby, a small-town north of Stockholm. The incident damaged the testimony of *Pingst* and other charismatic groups, becoming the most publicized news about the movement in the last fifty years.[116] The incident was investigated multiple times over the years, leading the church to leave the denomination of *Pingst*. While this was an isolated event, the damage lingers, and it can be

---

114. Stiernstedt, "10 År I Sverige."
115. Asker, "Gud Ett Måste."
116. Ringkvist, "Det Går Inte."

felt simply by mentioning it in conversation. Certainly, this occurrence did not present *Pingst* churches in a positive light.

Negative media attention on *Pingst* also resulted from the financial bankruptcy of the unequivocally heralded *Karisma* Center, which closed in 2005. The church strove to have a balanced approach to the five-fold ministry of the church with personnel employed to work in the areas of apostle, prophet, evangelist, shepherd, and teacher.[117] The hope of the church was to reach greater secular Stockholm alongside *Filadelfiakyrkan*, or *Filadelfia* Church. What occurred in their success, however, was that the pastors grew embarrassed by the small numbers of people coming to faith, leading them to exaggerate for reporting's sake. An investigation revealed that the location cost much money, as did the ministry events planned, which led to overspending.

All of this placed a burden on the church to aggregate more income, leading them to speak about finances far more than they had hoped in starting the Pentecostal church. Eventually, they would blame the United States and their modeling of charismatic churches. The implosion of *Karisma* Center unfolded through the secular media outlets, leading to a widening gap of trust between Swedish culture and Christian churches, and particularly, *Pingst* churches. As a result of these widely publicized blemishes across Swedish media, Pentecostal expressions of pneumatological activity became increasingly irrelevant in the perception of Swedish culture.

Perception of Pingst

Occasionally, Swedish newsprint editorials investigate the origin of Swedish holidays such as Pentecost, aptly named *Pingst*. The meaning of the Christian holiday is far removed from the meaning attached to the denomination of *Pingst*. This divide is attributed to a reinterpretation of the divine occurrence to apply to Swedish culture. As it pertains to the Day of Pentecost, when the baptism in the Holy Spirit accompanies speaking in tongues, secular Swedes distance themselves from this activity. Ironically, Swedes nationally observe the day of *Pingst* as *Pingstdagen*. Editorials offer the Swedish holiday of *Pingst* as a time to go for a walk, to fall in love, and to find people of one's own language to be around during the holiday.[118] Further, another editorial uses the idea of the *Pingst* holiday to describe the diversity amongst peoples in Sweden and their collective identity as Swedes, who can pop the

---

117. Sandberg, "En Stark Ekonomi."
118. Holmberg, "Lär Dig Konsten."

cork off of some wine and relax together.[119] Swedes treat *Pingst* as a metaphor and day off from work rather than as a divine event that exemplifies God's generosity and power.

On Speaking in Tongues

Swedish media questions the act of speaking in tongues. While the action of the *tungomålstal*, or speaking in tongues, and setting of the *kyrka*, or church, are the places where this pneumatological phenomena happens, the SSH doubts its divine origins.[120] Daniel Söderqvist, for example, has written about how a *Pingst* preacher speaks in tongues, "Raggavagga kakkala raggavagga kakkalaka . . ." He notes how the congregation follows suit, writing, "Kikkikra fassallo buloks . . ."

He questions why more people are not responding to spoken tongues and recognizing their own language. Further, he wonders how encouraging it would be to vacation in a foreign land and encounter someone speaking a clear message in Swedish. Editorials such as these illustrate how the mystery of the baptism in the Holy Spirit is not immune from being scrutinized. *Pingst* pastors and congregants consider this spiritual activity as direct communion with God, yet humanists regard it as an act rooted in humanity rather than divinity.

Perception of Healing

The Swedish media has documented little about divine healing. Any perspectives shared about this pneumatological activity tend to only be shared locally by the church on social media. Secular media disregards these occurrences. If someone claims to be healed, media attributes this not to divine intervention but to medical/technological breakthrough.[121] In other instances, Christians who pray for healing may have documented these events with Swedish doctors. True to their secular roots, however, Swedish Christians have called charismatic healing meetings "fake" and believe that ministers at these meetings cheat people into thinking that they are healed by God.[122] A general distrust in the validity of the event of divine healing is seated firmly in Swedish thought processes.

119. Schulman, "Tungor Såsom Av Eld."
120. Söderqvist, "Raggavagga Kakkala Raggavagga."
121. Byström, "Han Botades Från Diabetes."
122. Ottestig, "Helad Av Gud."

Naturalism Takes Over Spirituality

In the mind of an SSH, the practicality offered by reliance upon tangible phenomena remains more favorable than trusting in their spiritual origin. The unseen world has not given evidence enough for a Swede to regard spiritual activities as influential or substantial. The accumulation of social, cultural, historical, economic, and linguistic Swedish influence impacts the hermeneutic of the Swedish person.[123] Time and space replaces the providence and presence of God in Swedish culture.[124] Science supplants symbolism for explaining the inexplicable.[125] Further, the religious validity of God in Swedish culture has lost its credibility, aside from clergy who may still believe in Christ. Priests and marginal individuals who do believe the Christian message consist of only a few in comparison to the masses who simply do not and believe that they cannot.[126] The general, overwhelming Swedish perception of pneumatological activity is that the manifestations are either void of power and influence, altogether false, or indicate some activity perceived as found across all religions.

Summary

The SSH values truth and understanding according to their worldview based in tangibility and commitment to human rights. A disregard of theology, prevalence of postmodern thought, and anthropological progression of secular culture leads to a regression of regard for supernatural activity in Sweden. The boundaries of belief in a deity, according to the SSH, point to a psychological withdrawal from a reality which rationally accounts for both heaven and earth. This couches the perspective of an SSH in the ubiquitous understanding of "what you see is what you get."

CONCLUSION

Secular humanism which originates from the historical and cultural formation of Sweden affects the general Swedish perception of pneumatological activity. The study of Swedish Secular Humanism reveals how SSH process pneumatological activity. Swedish society welcomes the *mångfald* (diversity)

---

123. Netland, *Encountering Religious Pluralism*, 290.
124. Gibbs, *In Name Only*, 169.
125. Berger, *Social Construction of Reality*, 131.
126. Berger, *Sacred Canopy*, 124.

of perspectives present in the country due to the pluralistic tendency of the culture. Preference for practicality and trust in the *Folkhemmet* removes the need to trust in a divine being, changing the perspective of belief to one of scientific explanation. The influence of humanism remains deeply engrained within the historical and cultural fiber of Sweden. Pneumatological activity, then, is interpreted with skepticism and indifference. For Swedish society to recognize these occurrences as gifts from God will prove nothing short of a miracle. However, engaging an SSH with an example of pneumatological activity in action may remain the most effective way to evangelize these people who disregard God's existence. Given the influence of SSH in Sweden, might their presence in Sweden have potentially affected the development of *Pingst* churches? How has perception of pneumatological activity potentially changed?

4

A Historical Overview of Pingst Archival Literature of Their Perceptions of Pneumatological Activity Related to Church Multiplication

IN CONSTRUCTING A THEORY of Pentecostal church multiplication, a review of biblical and missiological perspectives on the activity of the Holy Spirit reveals a cyclical process of disciple/church multiplication in which all believers may participate. Jesus Christ exemplifies the actions of sending, proclaiming, gathering, and developing disciples, and consequently Paul the apostle did as well.[1] Christ invites all who trust him to join into *missio Dei*.

This chapter examines factors which initiated the Swedish Pentecostal movement as well as the leadership of Lewi Pethrus in order to glean the foundational perceptions of *Pingst* of the activity of the Holy Spirit in church multiplication among the unchurched.

FACTORS THAT INITIATED PINGST AS A CHURCH PLANTING MOVEMENT

Within Pentecostalism, there prevails an explicit belief that the Holy Spirit is active in the faith community. The disciple/church multiplication cycle, fueled by the Holy Spirit, provides direction and empowerment to affect

---

1. Hesselgrave et al., *Planting Churches Cross-Culturally*, 59.

the believer in mission.² The Spirit assists people to recognize the unity and progressive revelation of God as found through the confirmation of his work in the Christian community.³

As a denomination, *Pingst* began in 1913 through the founding of churches that established a new archetype of faith community that parted from the orthodoxy, orthopraxy, and orthopathy practiced by other churches of the early 1900s.⁴ Consideration of the spiritual, ecclesial, economic, and social situation of Sweden in chapter 3 reveals sociocultural factors that have assisted in initiating *Pingst* as a movement.⁵ Engagement of society in church planting mission is a historical component of the denomination. As a renewal church movement, *Pingst* was formed because of a spiritual awakening that led to world and local mission.

Gathering: Spiritual Awakening

To foreshadow the denominational shift and birth of Pentecostal denominations globally, as well as *Pingst*, the Moravian Church sent missionaries with incredible efficacy in the late eighteenth century.⁶ By contemporary standards, the Moravian Church was small, yet the impact of their movement contributes as a factor that birthed *Pingst* through revivals and meetings. The Wesleyan and Methodist revival started as a result of this mission effort, which then propelled missionaries to work in teams, as St. Patrick had before in his evangelization of the Celts.⁷ The Moravians were compelled to mission, yet as a result of their patient evangelistic efforts, churches were formed by their converts.⁸ In Sweden, rational doubt would be calmed by the Moravian missionaries as many chose Christ in Sweden because of these efforts.⁹

Mission is a product of spiritual awakening, producing differing streams of engagement. A Swedish man inspired by the mission work of the Moravians, Lars Levi Laestadius, preached repentance and taught a strict form of morality alongside Lutheran liturgy to the Sami people in 1844. This work among the indigenous people of northern Sweden would result in deliverance from shamanism. Concurrently, the Holiness movement would

2. Pethrus, *Wind Bloweth*, 91.
3. Lewis, *Missiological Research*, 153.
4. Niebuhr, *Christ and Culture*, lv.
5. Josefsson, "Liv Och Över Nog," 28.
6. Johnstone, *Global Church*, 133.
7. Hunter, *Celtic Way of Evangelism*, 9.
8. Beaver, *Perspectives*, 244.
9. Robert, *Occupy until I Come*, 33.

be born out of Lutherans, Methodists, and Baptists who shared an emphasis on prayer, repentance, the baptism in the Holy Spirit, and mission.[10] Rapid occurrences of pneumatological activity of sending, preaching, gathering, and developing disciples drew empowered believers from older church structures towards new, small congregations in Scandinavia.

Proto-Pentecostals

Prior to the Azusa Street revival of 1906, contributions of itinerant preachers, as well as William Booth, A. T. Pierson, and T. B. Barratt, would accelerate the shift from Reformed and Protestant denominations toward a conglomerate of belief and praxis that may best be understood as Pentecostal. Throughout the plains of the United States, namely Minnesota, North Dakota, South Dakota, and Ohio, Pentecostal revival meetings reached and shifted thousands towards a charismatic expression of their faith in Christ.[11] These proto-Pentecostals, many of whom were Swedish emigrants, started newsletters, writing to their motherlands about their experiences. Their correspondence birthed out of the Pentecostal experiences included multiple references to the *Helige Andes Dop* or baptism in the Holy Spirit.[12] Among other Swedes seeking opportunities in America, Andrew Johnson, a contemporary of Barratt and Pethrus, participated in the repentance meetings in 1904 in Los Angeles, choosing Christ himself. He then intersected with the Azusa revival in 1906, was baptized in the Holy Spirit, then returned to Sweden.[13]

Prayer

Initiating a Pentecostal cycle of disciple/church multiplication in Sweden, the desire to seek and find God grew throughout the 1800s and stretched into the 1900s.[14] Successive spiritual awakenings and revivals led to a new emphasis on joining in God's mission.[15] Each of these awakenings began with prayer, which assists the believer to realize God's desire for the salvation of humankind.

---

10. Bundy, *Visions of Apostolic Mission*, 72.
11. Rodgers, *Northern Harvest*, 4.
12. Teasley, "Helgelse," 3; Forrest, "Guds Församling," 1.
13. Alvarsson et al., *Pingströrelsen*, 1:18.
14. Siyameta, *Return to Babel*, 169.
15. Johnstone, *Global Churchs*, 135.

The denomination of *Pingst* began as a Holiness movement of prayer focused on the new outpouring of the Spirit and on an eschatological goal: Christ's return. *Bön* (prayer) was what gathered and developed the desire of believers in the late 1800s to dare to send and proclaim Christ to the nations. The development of the church continued as they prayed and fasted together, seeking God for direction in where to be sent. This fulcrum of prayer is denoted in the pre-*Pingst* newsletter *Glöd från Altaret*.[16] Usage in the archives of the newsletter points out the prevalence of *förbön*, or praying for something to occur, which was a prayer for other people, lands, or for something to occur. The extension of prayer for others to receive what God can provide is a characteristic of Pentecostalism globally as well as in Sweden. (Rom 8:26-27).

Further, *trosbön*, or prayers of faith, were also documented in this holiness-inspired newsletter. The publication reported that the revival awakening "has now come."[17] Eschatological focus on Christ's return in the Holiness movement was passed on to *Pingst*, per Pethrus's initial book offering through *Filadelfia förlaget*, *Jesus Kommer*.[18] While the focus of this writing was not on a Pentecostal experience, i.e., the baptism in the Holy Spirit, the spread of this central Gospel message depended on the Spirit-empowered witness of those who *had* been baptized in the Holy Spirit. As in Acts 19:1-7, the gospel is the center of ministry (see chapter 2). Prayer precedes the missiological task. What catalyzes people to be sent in *Pingst* disciple/church multiplication can be attributed to prayer and waiting for Christ's empowerment found in the baptism in the Holy Spirit.

Baptism in the Holy Spirit

The *löftet*, or promise, of the Father that Pethrus would sing about in his ministry was that of the baptism in the Holy Spirit. Accompanied by wind, glossolalian occurrence, and fire, the empowerment that was experienced by those present in Acts 2 was readily understood and realized as the promise about which Jesus had spoken (Luke 24:45-49). Swedish Holiness understood this empowerment to serve the purpose of propulsion and authority to go and make disciples in the name of Jesus, driven by the same Spirit who inhabited Jesus Christ. Within prayer meetings in holiness groups, the baptism in the Holy Spirit was experienced through obedient waiting as the early disciples did in Acts 2.

16. Gustafsson, "Början, Glöd Från Altaret," 1.
17. Gustafsson, "Början, Glöd Från Altaret," 3.
18. Pethrus, "Jesus Kommer."

Holiness preachers who related to the beginning of *Pingst* through relationship and ministry took note of the changes in a believer once they were baptized in the Holy Spirit. It fills the heart with love for others and unifies believers, according to T. B. Barratt.[19] The function of this baptism in the Holy Spirit is for the apostolic function of the believer to be unearthed, sending them to the ends of the earth. Two perceptions are the result of Spirit baptism. Love for fellow humans is evident as well as a unifying goal across Christianity in common mission to the lost.

Unfortunately, the Spirit-baptism of the Holiness and young *Pingst* movement would be criticized for their practice of speaking in tongues by cessationist protestant and evangelical priests and pastors. Barratt recounted that he was in fellowship with believers who shared in the perspective of water baptism and communion yet "miss the community of the Spirit" because of their perspective that Pentecostals were not having a normative Christian experience. Further, other Christian print media pronounced the Spirit-baptized and tongues-speaking believers as having been unsuccessful in their efforts of evangelism.[20]

Coupled with a passionate understanding of the Great Commission, the baptism in the Holy Spirit provides love and zeal within the believer to fulfill the task set before them.[21] While in prayer, Lewi Pethrus, the future leader of *Pingst*, longed for the baptism in the Holy Spirit as others in his Holiness prayer group had experienced. Swedish believers traveled far and wide to visit prayer groups who believed in the baptism in order that they too might share in God's blessing as promised so long ago. The transcontinental work of the Spirit was not sequestered to the United States at Azusa, nor would it be sequestered to Stockholm at *Filadelfiakyrkan* with future pastor Pethrus.

Developing: Seeking a Conducive Church Structure

The newly discovered Pentecostal spirituality of Sweden provided opportunity for new fellowships to form.[22] A desire to seek God according to this new spirituality would not always find place within current accepted and contextualized faith communities.[23] Changes within individual believers in Swedish churches can be recognized on a macro level across denominations.

19. Barratt, "Början, Glöd Från Altaret," 5.
20. Erik Andersen, "Början, Glöd Från Altaret," 13.
21. Johnson, *Apostolic Function*, loc. 226.
22. Pethrus, *Spiritual Memoir*, 14.
23. Hiebert, "Critical Contextualization," 109.

As a result, Fennoscandians began to search for different opportunities to worship alongside others who shared in their experience. Swedes baptized in the Holy Spirit did exhibit new boldness in their evangelistic efforts. While Swedish Pentecostals lived out their calling, the affinity to their Swedish rituals, traditions, and perspectives was still intact. Separate social groupings within Pentecostals, Baptists, and Lutherans exhibit similar traits to the whole of what was known as Swedish Christianity.[24] The Pentecostal awakening of some parishioners within the existing Methodist, Baptist, Catholic, and Lutheran congregations had brought about a dissatisfaction with their current ecclesial structure.[25][26] Seeking a separate expression of faith and devotion, while honoring the roots of one's faith, resulted in the birth of new churches being planted.

Swedish Pentecostals believe that their Spirit-empowered witness to the world aligns with the theology of the Luke/Acts literature with focus on the experience and patterns found regarding Spirit baptism. In Acts, the baptism in the Holy Spirit led to local and global evangelism followed by churches planted.[27] The resulting churches drew believers and unbelievers towards a way to live in communion with God alongside others (Rom 8:16–17). God's Spirit, as active in the sending, proclaiming, gathering, and development of the church, would form *Pingst* and send missionaries to Sweden's metaphorical Jerusalem, Judea, and Samaria, and to the ends of the earth.

Sending: Azusa to the World, Skövde to Sweden

The effect of the Azusa meetings spread all over the world wherever believers traveled. Andrew Johnson's return to Skövde, Sweden, is one of several places where speaking in tongues, interpretation, and prophecy accompanied Pentecostal expressions of prayer. These *böneringar*, or prayer circles, would pray day and night for the salvation of the towns where they lived. No more than eight to twelve people would be found at these house meetings, yet their effect would be felt through the empowered witness of those present.[28]

Johnson started house prayer meetings with the hopes that the Holy Spirit would send people per his own experience at Azusa. Soon after the

24. Niebuhr, *Social Sources of Denominationalism*, 22.
25. Halldorf, *Pentecostal Politics in a Secular World*, 37–55.
26. Erikson and Erikson, *Life Cycle Completed*, 54.
27. Beaver, *Perspectives*, 604.
28. Menzies, *Empowered for Witness*, 178.

meetings started, the Elim Baptist Church invited them to come and share within their walls. Following this opportunity, pastors from near and far in Sweden made the trip to Skövde to help decide if this "was from God or not."[29] Truly, the phenomena were from God and would inspire other churches. Of note, many Baptists sought the baptism of the Holy Spirit. John Ongman, from Örebro, was invited to work alongside Johnson to establish a strong Pentecostal presence that would transform and begin many churches throughout Sweden.[30] The foundation of the work in Örebro would find a home in Stockholm, in the initial name of Seventh Baptist Church, eventually becoming *Filadelfia* church, which would be home to thousands of parishioners. There would be a combination of changes in society that would provide opportunity for ministry to the cities of Sweden by the newly formed Pentecostal Church. As a result of the interaction of the church with society, congregations grew.

World Mission

What characterized the Holiness movement in its Pentecostal expression would be the way it would reach out to the countryside, as showcased in the ministry of Pethrus (to follow) and in its sending of missionaries to the ends of the earth. As the Moravians were sent two by two to share the gospel, modeled after Jesus's sending of the twelve and seventy-two disciples. The simple model that Pethrus observed among the Moravians affected him, enabling him to see opportunity for mission within Sweden. Further, modern mission in Sweden is heavily influenced by the Holiness missionary James Hudson Taylor, who established the China Inland Mission (CIM). The organization of CIM did not maintain its Pentecostal Spirit-baptized foundation. Taylor opened conversations regarding support with mainline Scandinavian church leaders about his ethos behind his model of Spirit-empowered model of sending people in mission.[31]

The Spirit motivates gathering of believers in fellowship (Acts 2:42–45). The "community of the Spirit," per Barratt, is the place where believers ask the Spirit where and to whom missionaries should be sent (13:2; 15:28). God's usage of humans to spread the gospel to the world from Sweden would reveal his heart for Brazil through two Swedish missionaries who would receive financial support from the Örebromissionen, *Pingst*'s first mission sending base. The model that Örebromission utilized was a hybrid of

29. Alvarsson et al., *Pingströrelsen*, 1:22.
30. Alvarsson et al., *Pingströrelsen*, 1:23.
31. Bundy, *Visions of Apostolic Mission*, 82.

Taylor's Pentecostalness as well as the establishment of a non-profit *förening* organization, which was apart yet connected to the church. Through mission efforts by Pentecostals in *Pingst*, people in Estonia, Brazil, Russia, and Congo have heard the gospel. This first mission base committed itself not only to world missions, but to reaching Sweden as well.

Local Mission

The Pentecostal *rörelse*, or movement, started through people like Johnson traveling abroad and in country. Stockholm, as a capital city, offered trade routes as well as a great base for industry to develop during the late industrial era of 1860–1910. Scientific institutes opened in central Stockholm, including the Karolinska medical facility. Interest in the city was a centripetal force, drawing in rural inhabitants of Sweden to seek work and fortune in the new economically advanced state.[32]

The modernization and urbanization of Sweden, in tandem with the centralization of governmental development, would establish diverse affinity groups.[33] Smaller Swedish communities ascribed relational roles to children rather than allowing for negotiation through achievement. As children became young adults, the allure of a more urban life appealed to them. In cities, however, young adults could chase these dreams without obligation to the relationships that tied them down in their small towns.[34] While some Pentecostals remained in a rural context, many moved to cities; their evangelistic efforts, driven by the Holy Spirit, founded faith communities in northern and southern Stockholm, Göteborg, and in other urban centers.[35]

Relief Efforts and the Disciple/Church Multiplication Cycle

To provide effective care for the poor and the refugee, Lewi Pethrus followed the example of the Salvation Army. Biblical principles can be found in his approach to caring for the poor, which coincide with the four phases of action exemplified by Jesus and Paul in the Cycle of Disciple/Church: proclaiming, gathering, developing, and sending.

---

32. Rojas, *Sweden after the Swedish Model*, 7.
33. Witoszek and Trägårdh, *Culture and Crisis*, 85.
34. Tamez, *Return to Babel*, 77.
35. Moberg, *Charismatic Christianity in Finland*, 8.

A Historical Overview 73

Urbanization: The Cities of Sweden

Within these movements of urbanization was the utilization of rural participants to produce goods and further pieces of the infrastructure. From 1780 to 1850, the proletariat (working) class formed. In times of recession, fifty percent of the total population were then considered poor.[36] The Salvation Army would be one of the first Christian-based organizations to return to the role of medical and humanitarian care for the poor, after this which was stripped from the Swedish Lutheran Church in 1860 by the Swedish government. They would establish bases in Värnamo as well as eastern Stockholm, renovating existing theatres and buildings to care for the poor.[37]

This evangelistic effort would be a precursor, paving the way for the work of Lewi Pethrus in providing relief for refugees and the poor, as well as the work which would occur in Södermalm of southern Stockholm. Soup kitchens opened in the basement of the *Filadelfia* church and in other Pentecostal churches around the city. Converts to Christ were born out of the poor, who ministered to and learned firsthand what it felt like to be without and then assist others in the hope that they could join in common mission.[38]

Proclaiming

Jesus Christ crossed cultures entering homes and traveling to those in need, meeting them at their place of pain. He did allow others to approach him as well, and even had instances recorded where he never needed to meet those who would be relieved of their pain (Matt 8:13). He also met many people in the midst of travels. He met the woman at the well (John 4), despite the shame and fear she may have felt as one ousted from society. Pethrus, along with a contingent of people from the *Filadelfia* church, received Finnish families at their point of arrival to the capital city of Stockholm.[39] They sought to relieve the acute stress of the poor as soon as possible.[40] Sharing the gospel and praying for the baptism in the Holy Spirit with those in crises provided hope and perception of a future to the downtrodden.

---

36. Dahlbäck and Nilsson, *Staden på Vattnet*, 189.
37. Salvation Army, "Salvation Army—Sweden."
38. Bundy, "Social Ethics," 2.
39. Pethrus, "En Kontingent Flyktingar," 60.
40. Puranen, "WV6 Results Sweden 2011."

The Swedish model of welfare, established in 1860, provides welfare for the poor. Government-provided care, however, can insulate a person from the personal contact that Jesus and Pethrus modeled in ministry. An added importance must be expressed that serving Jesus Christ supersedes all ties and loyalties when doing good.[41] Additionally, receiving those of like belief may be of interest to church leaders, yet the emphasis was primarily to "love your neighbor as yourself" (Mark 12:31). Satisfying the initial need of the refugee to receive personal attention would be the first step towards a relationship in which one becomes a disciple in Jesus Christ.

Gathering

Within each situation of ministry, Jesus engaged people at their point of human need. Through Jesus Christ's incarnational approach to relieving people, he healed the sick (Matt 20:32), put minds at ease (12:22), and fed myriads of people despite scarcity of food (14:13–21). He allowed those relieved to respond to their new circumstance. The healed would dance and tell others; the sane would share of their right minds; and ten thousand people would see that God provided a new type of manna for them (Exod 16:4). Pethrus, after receiving Finnish refugees in 1940 who had nothing but the clothes on their back, brought them to the central *Filadelfiakyrkan* building for rest, counsel, and food.[42] From this point on, the refugees were housed in family or communal homes connected to the church. Their encounter with Jesus's followers would change their perspective while their Swedish caretakers would earn their trust.

Developing

Jesus Christ spoke regularly with his disciples, challenging them with questions. After satisfying their needs and earning their trust, Jesus then left them with the quandary of his identity. Experiencing the effects of Jesus's love prompted a question to the relieved refugee that would be like what Jesus asked Peter: "Who do you say I am?" (Mark 8:29). Pethrus and his congregation revealed that their actions towards the refugees were motivated by God's love.[43] This disclosure revealed why one would be compelled to help another. As evidenced from the *Evangelii Herald*, refugees

---

41. Park, *Ministry to Migrants*, loc. 205.
42. Pethrus, "En Kontingent Flyktingar," 60.
43. Pethrus, "En Kontingent Flyktingar," 80.

assisted by Pethrus either became believers themselves or were believers that evangelized others. Pethrus regularly encouraged his church members to exhibit the Pentecostal promise of the baptism in the Holy Spirit as a sign "to them that believe not."[44] Receiving the poor, then, became a viable avenue for making disciples to send as missionaries (Matt 28:18–20).

Summary

Pentecostal factors contributing to *Pingst* church multiplication include prayer, baptism in the Holy Spirit, and the formation of missionary sending organizations. While a strong parallel exists between Swedish expression and that of the early church of Acts 2, culture affects the development of the church, providing unique expressions of governance and foci for mission. While there was a diversity of Christians that followed the awakenings, Pentecostal expressions gather believers to participate in the biblical pathway of being sent, proclaiming, gathering, and developing disciples throughout Sweden. *Pingst* would find that sources feeding their movement would need to find form as they already exhibited a function to send and empower servants across Sweden. Through the presence of dissatisfied Christians, the spiritual awakening taking place, as well as the urbanization and establishment of Christianity in the poorer classes, *Pingst* found the leadership necessary for their movement in Lewi Pethrus. As a friend once told me, "To study *Pingst* and its beginnings is to study Pethrus."[45]

CONTRIBUTION OF LEWI PETHRUS TO PERCEPTION OF PNEUMATOLOGICAL ACTIVITY

The Spirit of God inhabits and assists believers in service to others. This foundational understanding resides in the legacy of Lewi Pethrus. The formation of Pethrus's focused vision originates from his theology of salvation and Spirit baptism. His influence and leadership assisted the formation of the Swedish Pentecostal movement, *Pingst*. The Pentecostal, church-planting perspective that he employed empowered *Pingst* towards the evangelization of all Swedish cities and towns. This section researches the origin and implementation of Lewi Pethrus's Pentecostal ecclesial outreach.

---

44. Pethrus, *A Spiritual Memoir*, 39.
45. Sjöström, interview.

Pethrus's Christianity

Pethrus grew up in the village of Vargön, where he lived in the same house until he turned fifteen years old. His parents afforded him a quiet childhood in which he found the deciduous and pine forests to be not only his playground but also his place to contemplate his Christian faith.[46] Following the guidance of his mother and father, he remained serious in his pursuit of God and had grown attuned to existential questions quite early in his life.[47] As a young adult, he moved away from home to the western city of Vänersborg, near the coast that borders Norway. Pethrus began working at a shoe factory among hundreds of others from the *kommun*, or township.

Proclaiming and Gathering: Pethrus Responds to the Gospel

At the church in Vänersborg, Pethrus was baptized and committed his life to Christ in 1899. He responded to the proclamation of the gospel and found himself in the company of a church that sought God. Pethrus felt a desire to serve God, a calling confirmed by a friend's father, Varner Högberg, who challenged him to become a preacher. Further exploring his orientation towards the Holy Spirit, he sought the assistance of his Baptist pastor, who informed him of the cessation of the Spirit.[48] However, this perspective did not stop Pethrus from seeking more of God. While living in close quarters with two roommates, Pethrus began his preaching ministry by witnessing to them in their apartment. He sought the power he had read about in the Acts of the Apostles, noting the revived outlook on life discussed in the Scriptures.[49]

Pethrus continued to seek God and assisted in preaching in Sweden and Norway. In 1902, after an all-night prayer meeting on the island of Lillesand, off the coast of Norway, Pethrus experienced the baptism of the Holy Spirit while traveling home by ferry.[50] No one else witnessed the experience, and no worship service was underway when this happened. Pethrus doubted that this baptism had occurred because of the normality of the setting despite the strong connection he felt with God.[51] Transformed but not displaying the accompanying manifestation of speaking in tongues,

---

46. Pethrus, *Spiritual Memoir*, 15.
47. Janson, "Lewi Pethrus På Vargön."
48. Pethrus, *Spiritual Memoir*, 17.
49. Pethrus, *Wind Bloweth*, 15.
50. Janson, "Lewi Pethrus På Vargön."
51. Pethrus, *Spiritual Memoir*, 25.

Pethrus continued in ministry. Pethrus's heart continued to seek opportunities to serve God and to learn more about him from the Scriptures and from people of like mind.

One such person Pethrus consulted was Norwegian Methodist minister T. B. Barratt, who encountered the baptism in the Holy Spirit because of his travels in the United States in November 1906.[52] Upon returning the next month, Barratt began revival meetings in Oslo,[53] which Pethrus heard about through newspaper articles.[54] Many pastors went to observe the meetings, treating them as phenomena to be researched.[55] Pethrus traveled to Oslo in 1907 to participate in the meetings as he felt his Christian life lacking in power despite his baptism in the Holy Spirit in 1902. Pethrus answered the invitation for prayer given at the front of the Baptist Tabernacle Church one evening, and Barratt prayed for him. After realizing he had already received the baptism in the Holy Spirit five years earlier, Pethrus took comfort in how God had met him with his initial experience. This moment would prove integral to the church planting ministry Pethrus would later have.

In addition to the prayer, Barrett asked him three questions that stoked his resolve to be of service to God: "Would you be anything for God? Would you do anything for God? Would you go anywhere for God?"

Developing: Personal and Spiritual Formation

The spiritual formation of Lewi Pethrus answers the first question of Barratt's challenge. From an early age, Pethrus understood the importance of giving his life to God. His hometown knew him as being the youngest to experience a believer's baptism by immersion in the Baptist church at age fifteen.[56] He lived his life with a divine passion, saying, "If everyone else is giving their lives to something, then I will throw myself entirely to what God has for me."[57] His study habits, work ethic, and dedication to the church were set in place within his first twenty years of life.

---

52. Alvarsson et al., *Pingströrelsen*, 1:17.
53. Then known as *Kristiania*.
54. Bundy, *Visions of Apostolic Mission*, 171.
55. Pethrus, *Spiritual Memoir*, 26.
56. Carlsson, *Människan, Samhället, Och Gud*, 28.
57. Janson, "Lewi Pethrus På Vargön."

Autonomy

In reference to Swedish culture, anthropologists conclude that for a citizen to participate in Swedish culture, one must demonstrate autonomy.[58] Pethrus established that he belonged to the work of God, his way of standing on his "own two feet."[59] Once he left home, he also decided that he wanted to change his birth name from Levi to Lewi, perhaps as a marker of his newfound autonomy. His given name of Levi possessed a biblical gravity to it, and much of what he did, he did individually. He sought God on his own in his youth and experienced God alone as an older man. He surrounded himself in ministry with his friends, yet he established his own personal conviction and care for the Lord, which helped build God's Kingdom.[60] He knew that people fail, but his promises do not. His outlook made him an exemplary leader in both the context of Sweden and the church.

Lewi Pethrus served as an entrepreneur, one who sought to master all things related to the service of the church. He wrote sermons, learned to play instruments, wrote songs, created organizational structure, and developed theology. Known as a strong, conservative leader, his Swedish individualism found new ground within the leadership structure of the church, further creating a prominent profile of himself in Swedish society. The centralized government structure of the country is not conducive to the development of nonprofit, volunteer organizations, but this context elevated the potency of Pethrus's witness.[61] His relationship with God remained central to his life. He placed great responsibility on each Christian to establish a solid relationship with God, exemplified by saying, "Drink water out of your own fountain which God supplies."[62]

Family

Pethrus learned from his family how to create space in which to explore God's purposes for himself and his relatives. His mother would read from the Psalms each new year to establish a song for the family, one they would focus on during the next year.[63] Dedicated believers, his parents raised their children in the faith. As a father himself, Pethrus did not parent harshly. He

---

58. Berggren and Trägårdh, *Är Svensken Människa?*, 48.
59. Carlsson, *Människan, Samhället, Och Gud*, 29.
60. Carlsson, *Människan, Samhället, Och Gud*, 28.
61. Trägårdh, *Society in Northern Europe*, 128.
62. Janson, "Lewi Pethrus På Vargön."
63. Carlsson, *Människan, Samhället, Och Gud*, 300.

gave his children latitude to ask questions and play, and he did not hassle them to leave on time for church on Sunday mornings.[64] If he became angry at work, it seldom followed him home in how he treated his family.[65] He strove to bring his children up to follow Christ. Of the nine children he and his wife Lydia parented, only one left the church.[66] As a calm father, Pethrus allowed his children the opportunity to grow, ask questions, and begin their faith in Christ.

In love, his wife Lydia and he shared various difficulties and triumphs during their marriage. The experience of Pethrus's baptism in the Holy Spirit caused the newly courting couple to temporarily stop their relationship so that Lewi could focus all of his efforts on what God was calling him to do at the time.[67] After four and a half years in service at the Baptist church in Linköping, the newly formed *Filadelfia* church in Stockholm called him to pastor their twenty members. He purposed himself to grow the church to a size that could financially support him as the pastor and enable him to support his future family. When *Filadelfia* had grown to five hundred members and had become financially stable, Pethrus wrote to Lydia, who had moved to the United States to pursue education. She accepted his invitation and they married.

In 1929, Lydia became gravely ill. While the church prayed for her, Pethrus experienced a moment of crisis in which he had lost all hope. Then twenty-nine years old, he began to write a song, which served as an exposé of himself. *Löftena kunna ej Svika* spoke of God's promise of steadfastness, which could withstand the most disastrous of events.[68] Further, the promise that had propelled him was that of the baptism in the Holy Spirit. With no words to populate his prayers, he relied on God's promises on behalf of his family. Pethrus stated that the song lacked creativity and did not need deep interpretation. He simply grieved for his beloved and connected the events to God. As Lydia returned to health, the song became a staple of the *Filadelfia* congregation, born out of deep love for his wife.[69] Common knowledge accentuated the loving marriage that Lewi and Lydia had; even novelists compared their wedlock to others as a standard for Sweden.[70]

---

64. Norén, "Lewi Pethrus Ättlingar Samlas I Nora I Dag."
65. Therese Peterson, "Vem Var Han?"
66. Norén, "Lewi Pethrus Ättlingar Samlas I Nora I Dag."
67. Pethrus, *Spiritual Memoir*, 29.
68. Pethrus, "Löftena Kunna Ej Svika."
69. Janson, "Lewi Pethrus På Vargön."
70. Enquist, *Lewi's Journey*, 171.

Church

When asked why he wanted to be known as a Christian, Pethrus replied, "I am called a Christian because through baptism, I am now a part of the church of Jesus Christ."[71] This declaration unearths the connection between a public profession of faith and the assimilation of the believer into a sociological grouping who identify with Jesus Christ. When others criticized Pethrus for his sermons or writings, his children wondered how he could withstand the opposition. When criticism arose against the church, Pethrus responded with a forceful temperament, ranging from strong rebukes, to publicly calling out dishonesty, to outright anger.[72] While he sometimes lacked empathy, his primary concern was that the church would retain its purity as the bride of Christ.[73] Apart from Lewi Pethrus, there has not existed a more exhaustive contribution to written Swedish Pentecostal theology in writing. His love for the church developed his capacity as a leader for the *Filadelfia* church and to the wider *Pingst* fellowship.

Sending: Pethrus and His Pentecostal Influence

Both a theorist and practitioner, Pethrus felt driven to give God glory through his formulation of thought and creed, as well as through the actions of the church.[74] Pethrus had experienced life within Holiness prayer circles, which existed throughout Norway and Sweden.[75] He saw the need for more than a denominational organization; he knew Christians needed to be formed and mobilized.[76] Through Pethrus's leadership, many people from the Holiness movement became the congregants of the Pentecostal churches he formed as a part of *Pingst*.

Pethrus and the Baptism in the Holy Spirit

Only Pethrus's love for his family and his love for God superseded his love for the church. He understood the baptism of the Holy Spirit as an

---

71. Carlsson, *Människan, Samhället, Och Gud*, 28.

72. Gäreskog and Gäreskog, *Lewi Pethrus I Konflikt*, 35, 144; Norén, "Ättlingar Samlas I Nora."

73. Pethrus, *Christian Church Discipline*, 39.

74. Fowler, *Stages of Faith*, 93.

75. Halldorf, ""En Församling I Varje Stad," 40.

76. Alvarsson et al., *Pingströrelsen*, 1:38.

equipping for service to God.[77] As a Baptist minister, he felt uneasy within the denominational structure because of his experience, so he continued to seek those of like mind. The growth of the church structure relied upon the Pentecostal distinctive as a shared experience amongst congregants.[78]

Pethrus proposed that baptism should remain a normative part of the Christian experience.[79] The Holiness movement, which preceded the denominational organization *Pingst*, enabled Pethrus to meet others already practicing the baptism in the Holy Spirit. Later in his ministry, *Filadelfia* church hosted an American boys' choir from Youth for Christ. Before leaving Sweden, a group of boys, which included a young Billy Graham, asked Pethrus for the secret to his success, to which he replied, "The baptism in the Holy Spirit."[80] As he sought God for this promised gift, he gave himself in service to God as he pastored the largest church in Scandinavia and later launched a church planting movement.

New doctrines would form within the new groups of proto-Pentecostals.[81] In 1907, Pethrus learned that he had been baptized in the Holy Spirit five years earlier, although he was looking for a more pronounced experience. The setting where God met him occurred in nature, where he experienced it alone and without music or worship from any other voice. This baptism experience changed the paradigm of ministry in which he lived, illuminating the nature of God's omnipresence. Between 1902 and 1907, Pethrus recounts that he did not practice the continuing experience of Spirit baptism.[82] This realization of the necessity to maintain a connection to God through the gift of baptism convicted Pethrus to exercise his faith as often as possible.

The Baptist denomination based in Stockholm clearly encouraged those who participated in the new movement to start their own organization.[83] In response, Pentecostals retained friend and familial connections among church members who disregarded the baptism in the Holy Spirit. This approach closely followed the proliferation of existing and newly planted churches claiming to be Pentecostal while maintaining a cordial relationship with the Baptists. At the same time, the new groups demanded some form of organization to give structure to their blossoming fellowship.

77. Pethrus, *Wind Bloweth*, 20.
78. Nida, *Customs and Cultures*, 37.
79. Pethrus, *Wind Bloweth*, 19.
80. Pethrus, *Spiritual Memoir*, 19.
81. Niebuhr, *Social Sources of Denominationalism*, 21.
82. Hartwick, "Enrichment Journal."
83. Alvarsson et al., *Pingströrelsen*, 1:38.

However, the Baptists cited open communion as the reason for the separation of the Pentecostal churches from theirs.[84]

Editorial Work

Through his writings, Pethrus garnered the attention of Pentecostal churches. His initial *insändare* (editorial) to the *Swedish Tribune* in 1910 proved memorable to leaders throughout Sweden, one that elicited a notation in Barratt's diary because of the gravity of his words. The following year, Pethrus was invited to pastor Seventh Baptist Church in Stockholm, which would later be renamed *Filadelfia* church. Alongside his new work as a pastor, a new Pentecostal newsletter from Stockholm, the *Brudgummans Röst* (*The Groom's Voice*), asked him to serve as editor. The newsletter provided an outlet for the new movement to discuss the experience, meaning, and function of the baptism of the Holy Spirit. It also provided space for debate as Sweden's egalitarian societal formation gave rise to many voices who wished to contribute to and support the new movement.[85]

Pethrus maintained his editorial work for the Pentecostal network with the *Brudgummans Röst* and began a newsletter for *Filadelfia* church called *Evangelii Härold*.[86] In the early iterations of the paper, he used ad space to encourage new readers of *Härold* to read the *Röst* as well[87].

Extensive use of the words, *Helige Ande*, Holy Spirit, and *tungotal*, speaking in tongues, confirm the Pentecostal emphasis of Pethrus and other Pentecostal pastors in the writing. As he shared his writings from the *Härold* within the widely circulated *Röst*, he found himself at odds with the other leaders of the Pentecostal newsletter. Rather than humble himself, he cut ties with *Brudgummans Röst* and focused on his own paper. It should be noted that the idea of the *Evangelii Härold*[88] was likened to a publication found amongst Swedish proto-Pentecostals in Minnesota entitled *Evangelii Trumpet*.[89] Pethrus's focus on the local church and its power served as the means for reaching the world. For example, Pethrus invited Daniel Berg, childhood friend and missionary to Brazil, to have a singular supporting church in *Filadelfia* rather than draw funds from the larger Pentecostal movement.[90]

84. Carlsson, *Människan, Samhället, Och Gud*, 32.
85. Pethrus, "Brudgummans Röst."
86. Alvarsson et al., *Pingströrelsen*, 1:41.
87. Gustaffsson, "Brudgummans Röst Annonsering," 4.
88. *Härold* is Swedish for trumpet.
89. Forrest, "Guds Församling."
90. Bundy, *Visions of Apostolic Mission*, 354.

Sermons and Books

Pethrus entitled his first sermon series at *Filadelfia* church "*Jesus Kommer*" ("Jesus Is Coming"). Similar to how A. T. Pierson's end times-focused sermons were written for distribution, Pethrus discovered that his theology would motivate and send people to the ends of the earth.[91] This title echoed Pethrus's propensity to emphasize eschatological thought as a motivating factor in his own life. Various Pentecostal newsletters would highlight parts of his series. As interest grew from readers, the sermon series was then advertised as a book sold at the *Filadelfia* church's own bookstore.[92]

Pethrus put his sermons to manuscript so that the transfer to written books would be seamless, enabling the distribution of his messages for reading and learning. Following his example of preserving sermons in books, the current pastor of *Filadelfia* church, Niklas Piensoho, wrote *100 dagar med Jesus*. In addition to the book, Piensoho developed a sermon series and video campaign.[93]

Governing

Pethrus saw the unity of the church as a strength and published a work about its ecclesiological importance.[94] One church would grow to be strong in its identity, vision, ideals, and practice, yet it would remain distinct as they no longer remained with the Baptist movement.[95] While Holiness groups around Sweden exercised an egalitarian approach to how they congregated, Pethrus created a structure that demonstrated quite the opposite. Fueled by the baptism in the Holy Spirit and enlightenment of thought, he built the church.[96] He sought to gather people to receive the message of Christ, albeit *his* interpretation of the message of Christ. His humility remained evident in his posture towards God, yet he displayed boldness as he envisioned *Filadelfia* church as a place where all should want to attend.

As a result, Pethrus took an authoritarian approach to leadership and decided most things himself. He elevated his leadership to the point that if a staff member inferred that *Filadelfia* church was not spiritually deep,

---

91. Robert, *Occupy until I Come*, 135.
92. Pethrus, "Jesus Kommer," 4.
93. Piensoho, *100 Dagar Med Jesus*.
94. Aronson, "Ecclesiology of Lewi Pethrus," 196.
95. Thörn, "En Framgångsrik Främling," 30.
96. Moore, *Kingdom of Christ*, 29.

he would terminate the staff member's employment the next day.[97] That mediation between God and humankind would occur as a built-in part of the hierarchy in which Pethrus held veto power proved apparent.[98]

Although the Pentecostal churches lacked a clarified structure of leadership, the fellowship viewed Pethrus as the spokesperson for the movement.[99] Not by formal designation but by effort and focus, Pethrus steered the fledgling church. He viewed Scripture as the primary guide for *Filadelfia* to exercise disciplinary measures. In every task, Pethrus sought a biblical understanding that he would then apply to Christian ideals for the Swedish people.[100] *Filadelfia*, along with other Pentecostal churches influenced from affiliation, benefited from the new ecclesial environment that Pethrus had created from 1913 to 1919, one which bore both the presence of God and the structure of Pethrus. Pethrus would refer to the church as an "assembly" or "congregation," yet he felt reluctant to form a denomination.[101]

Pethrus focused on glorifying God, something he believed would happen primarily through the local church. Film documentaries and his writings confirm that Pethrus understood the idea of *missio Dei* as he sought to further count the stars that Abraham began counting so many years ago.[102] This extension of God's work remained of utmost importance to Pethrus to the point that it challenged his Swedish citizenship. Civic participation remained important in the early 1900s, yet the church needed increased attention as it worked to emphasize salvation in Christ to people.[103] Lutheran and Baptist congregations of the day treated parishioners as consumers who visited and prayed, stewards of the church property and finances. Pethrus, however, viewed the church as a resource of participants in mission.[104] The centralized structure of Sweden heavily influenced the centralized structure of *Filadelfia* and the surrounding Pentecostal churches. One strong difference, though, persisted between the Swedish context and the burgeoning Pentecostals: Sweden had an ornamental monarchy with a functional parliament while *Filadelfia* had both a functional monarchy and a parliament.[105]

97. Alvarsson et al., *Pingströrelsen*, 1:81.
98. Wildavsky, *Nursing Father*, 24.
99. Gäreskog and Gäreskog, *Lewi Pethrus I Konflikt*, 23.
100. Pethrus, *Christian Church Discipline*, 12.
101. Aronson, " Ecclesiology of Lewi Pethrus," 195.
102. Carlsson, *Människan, Samhället, Och Gud*, 30; Janson, "Lewi Pethrus På Vargön."
103. McClung, *Globalization of Pentecostalism*, 30.
104. Trägårdh, *Society in Northern Europe*, 129.
105. Witoszek and Trägårdh, *Culture and Crisis*, 37.

Pethrus's Role as Founder of *Pingst*

The social structure of Sweden began to shift through the spiritual awakening promoted by Barratt, Pethrus, and others. As people moved and grouped themselves into small clusters throughout Sweden, Pethrus challenged Spirit-led believers to attend Bible studies and mission meetings in new locations.[106] Echoing the expansion of the early church, Swedish Pentecostals began to mobilize and spread. Although he was anti-denomination, Pethrus used his influence over the movement to form assemblies that would reach Sweden. Moreover, Pethrus did not target any particular social group but welcomed any who would repent.[107] After developing *Filadelfia* in Stockholm, Pethrus used the church as a model for ecclesial multiplication in other cities.

Training People for Ecclesial Outreach

Pethrus's heart centered on God's mission to reach people with the gospel of Jesus Christ. He confidently believed that the local church body served as the format for reaching people.[108] Central to Pethrus's belief system was that the baptism in the Holy Spirit existed as the reason for the new local movement, the one that would bring salvation to Sweden and make world missions possible.[109] Underscoring this spiritual shift and feeding the new movement of ecclesial outreach were the movements to train leaders, engage in social relief efforts in Stockholm, and separate and renew churches.

The process of starting churches required training people. Beginning in 1917, three-day training meetings occurred in Skövde, Luleå, Stockholm, Göteborg, and Malmö,[110] where preachers and evangelists would learn under the leadership of Pethrus and others.[111] This educational system largely borrowed from Pethrus's experience from the Baptist movement.[112]

As the movement grew into something that resembled a denomination, it would only be a matter of time before structure needed to be in place to help guide the willing participants receiving training. Many Baptists were leaving the Baptists in favor of the new Pentecostal movement. Spiritual growth was happening akin to the Swedish immigrants in Minnesota, who

---

106. Alvarsson et al., *Pingströrelsen*, 1:48.
107. Allen, *Missionary Methods*, 23.
108. Pethrus, *Christian Church Discipline*, 52.
109. York, *Missions in the Age of the Spirit*, 81.
110. Central, North, East, West, South, respectively.
111. Alvarsson et al., *Pingströrelsen*, 2:52.
112. Pethrus, *Spiritual Memoir*, 20.

became Pentecostal in the late 1800s.[113] Further, Sven Lidman, an experienced novelist, came to faith through the ministry of Pethrus. He noted that both rationalism and revival remain necessary for Christianity. His own salvation narrative proved instrumental in advertising through Swedish media that atheists would not be immune to the new movement led by Pethrus.[114] The gospel meant training and reaching people, a natural outgrowth of the spiritual perspectives of Pethrus and the *Filadelfia* church.

Social Work in Ecclesial Outreach

The work of *Filadelfia* Stockholm did not only provide for the spiritual salvation and development of Stockholm, it also allotted for the physical needs as well. The church's ministry outreach to homeless and unemployed Stockholmers included lodging and food distribution.[115] World War I left many without work, which contributed to the impoverished population of Sweden.[116] Further, the church assisted in fundraising efforts to provide for children's homes on the edges of Stockholm.[117] Later, during the beginning of both the Winter War and World War II, *Filadelfia* would meet refugees and children at the train station in Stockholm to guide them to the Sjöarp transitional home.[118] Pethrus would also send church members to assist infants and young children on the trains in an effort to provide them relief.[119] Endless opportunities for social relief came for the church to provide what Swedish society had left undeveloped. The work of the global church to care for the widows and orphans of a society is not only a litmus test for the church (Jas 1:27), it also qualifies as the ecclesial outreach of loving one's neighbor (Lev 19:18; Luke 10:29–37).

The *Filadelfia* church training of preachers and evangelists would inspire them to participate in revival throughout Sweden. This new wave of ecclesial outreach appeared as a Pentecostal awakening of the dormant apostolic Holiness people of Scandinavia, yet there existed a strong christological focus within the teaching.[120] Pethrus would speculate that there could have been both divine and socioeconomic reasons for

113. Rodgers, *Northern Harvest* 32.
114. Rodgers, "Prominent Novelist Sven Lidman."
115. Pethrus, "Filadelfiaförsamlingens I Stockholm," 2.
116. Alvarsson et al., *Pingströrelsen*, 2:52.
117. Lewi Pethrus, "Gåfvor Till Oscarsbergs."
118. Sjöberg, "Giv Fredens Helige Ande!," 1015.
119. Lewi Pethrus, "En Kontingent Flyktingar Från Finland," 60.
120. Davidsson, *Lewi Pethrus' Ecclesiological Thought*, 70.

the Pentecostal movement, yet their efforts would eventually result in a collective of churches seeking to become a denomination.

Given the Swedish Pentecostals' desire to learn in tandem with opportunities to serve Swedish communities in crises of faith and physical need, Pethrus began to move towards a unified system of ecclesial outreach that led to churches being planted in each city.[121] The model that many looked to for structure and mission was *Filadelfia* church, Pethrus's own congregation.

Paul as Example

In terms of the baptism of the Holy Spirit, Pethrus's spirituality and theology echoed the thoughts and work of Paul in his apostolicity, commitment, and demeanor. Whereas Paul remained far more mobile as he lived out the propagation of the gospel, Pethrus employed teams of people willing to go into Sweden and beyond.[122] Whether Paul traveled or Pethrus inspired others, the church expanded.[123] Paul traveled and evangelized in a variety of ways: alone, with companions, and through teams. The social group engaged in outreach vastly affected their degree of reach and impact.[124] Likewise, Pethrus sent and inspired groups of people to reach their communities through equipping those who heard and received their commission from God.[125] Paul also employed a strategy of church planting that first focused on sharing the message of Christ at the community's synagogue and then worked its way to the marketplace. This reflected the ministry approach of each Swedish community.

One Church per City

Perhaps the most notable phrase stated by Lewi Pethrus relates directly to ecclesial outreach—"one church in every city."[126] This statement earmarked the strategy that Pethrus employed in church planting.[127] Pethrus's entrepreneurial spirit borrowed from Swedish emigrants who had settled

121. Pope John Paul II, "Cor Unum."
122. Beggs, *Indigenous Principles*, 64.
123. Allen, *Spontaneous Expansion*, loc. 99.
124. Hunter, *Celtic Way of Evangelism*, 129.
125. Hiebert, " Flaw of the Excluded Middle," 483.
126. *En Församling i varje ort*.
127. Halldorf et al., *Församlingsplantering I Pingst*, 39.

in St. Paul Park, Minnesota. They employed the strategic concept of a singular entity reaching out to a singular entity.[128] What sets Pethrus apart from many other apostolic leaders, however, is that he was a theologian and a practitioner who closely lived what he preached. "One church per city" would give form and apostolic function to the new movement, further solidifying its future role as a denomination in Sweden.[129] Because Pethrus valued unity, he planned ecclesial outreach through multiple churches. To plant one church per city would require hub churches within larger cities throughout Sweden to plant preaching outposts in smaller cities. He would send pastors from larger churches in nearby urban centers, who would then send preachers to establish ministry outposts within smaller towns.

This hub model focused on the urban first and then the rural. The homogeneity of Swedish society provided an even canvas by which the newly charismatic Swedes would begin and renew congregations.[130] Spiritual hunger had become evident, yet the social conditions of homelessness, substance abuse, and unemployment remained consistent throughout various cities, towns, and villages.

Heavily influencing the push to reach every culture and provide them a local church is the appeal of closure, a concept broadly shared across mission agencies.[131] "Reaching the nations within this generation" was a common phrase spoken in conferences and preaching circles throughout the United States and Europe. The totality of Pethrus's resolve resulted in churches springing up near the urban centers of each town throughout Sweden. *Filadelfia* church's name would grow in influence and geographic breadth wherever Swedes settled, such as Chicago, Oslo, and Reykjavik. Though the social system of Sweden had long forgotten its roots of a confessional lifestyle, a resurgence of ministry, training, and sharing the gospel once again took hold in Sweden.[132]

The initial pioneering work of Pentecostal church planting— "one church per city"—had accomplished exactly what it had purposed itself to do. They had established the presence of the church where it did not exist.[133] This strategy proved effective for ecclesial outreach, yet over time, this methodology had become theology.[134]

128. Forrest, "Guds Församling."
129. Johnson, *Apostolic Function*, loc. 1053.
130. Johnstone, *Future of the Global Church*, 121.
131. Willowbrook, *Perspectives*, 517.
132. Pierson, *Dynamics of Christian Mission*, 142.
133. Halldorf et al., *Församlingsplantering I Pingst*, 45.
134. Sjöström, interview.

On Restriction

As the church spontaneously expanded in Sweden through a variety of ways, the movement that had begun through *Filadelfia* was understood through the lens of "one church per city."[135] At the same time, however, the phrase had also restricted its growth.[136] Roland Allen identifies fear as the primary reason the church imposes control on the uncontrollable work of the Spirit. At the time of the expansion of the church, Swedes, driven to survive, exhibited a high degree of risk-avoidance.[137] Unemployed Swedes, particularly during the stock market crash of 1929, devoted themselves to active organizations. The call for "one church per city" provided no space for ambiguity or uncertainty.[138] With *Filadelfia* church's profound influence, the shared mentality led people to only consider *Filadelfiakyrkan* model as the primary way to plant churches. Most believed that only one church could be allowed within the boundary of a city.[139] Pentecostals later assumed that disunity would arise, as Pethrus suggested, if any other church began in Stockholm alongside his work.

This mentality has perpetuated itself throughout the years, limiting church planting efforts. Pethrus condemned the acceptance of smaller congregations, citing their inability to collect large offerings: "It is fun to be a pastor of a large church who can take in a large offering and accomplish a meaningful task in one evening... a church of 15,000 to 20,000, this is what Stockholm needs."[140] The idea of multiple churches inhabiting a city meant disunity, something which was unacceptable to Pethrus as it would lead to ineffective ministry.[141]

When a change agent goes into a nearby town to establish a ministry outpost, there exists a possibility that a new and autonomous congregation will be born from the congregation that sent the missionary in the first place—the sharing of power.[142] Pethrus comfortably shared resources, so long as those sent were considered his people. He happily sent people, if they originated from his direction. Pethrus retained control, potentially restricting the growth of the movement because of his unwillingness to share

---

135. Halldorf, *Pentecostal Politics in a Secular World*, 192–95.
136. Allen, *Spontaneous Expansion of the Church*, 187.
137. Ögren, *Swedish Financial Revolution*, 90.
138. Hofstede et al., *Cultures and Organizations*, loc. 3289.
139. Halldorf et al., *Församlingsplantering I Pingst*, 49.
140. The church at the time had two hundred to three hundred members.
141. Lewi Pethrus, "Den Nytestamentliga Enhetstanken," 95.
142. Koeshall, *Redeemed Power*, 218.

power. Whether this hunger for control occurs within the city limits or not remains immaterial. It fell short of trying "to get people saved," according to William J. Seymour. Pethrus may have had a territorial approach to understanding church culture and organizational growth. Certainly, however, his drive to make disciples cannot be questioned.

The Role of the Holy Spirit in Church Planting in Early *Pingst*

Previously in this chapter, it was discovered that early *Pingst* writings by Pethrus and other authors relied on the Holy Spirit for their guidance as well as power for mission. The effects of the baptism in the Holy Spirit on the believers of Sweden changed their expression of their Christianity to include a focus on evangelism and inclusion of others in mission. The perspective of those within the *Pingst* movement believed that the promise of the Holy Spirit was meant for every believer. One of the greatest opportunities that *Pingst* utilized in sharing its theology throughout the network of churches in the early 1900s was through hymns and spiritual songs. "*Löftet kunna ej Svika*"[143] was written by Pethrus to encourage believers to trust the leading and empowerment of the Holy Spirit despite the environment around them.

The "one church per city" metric was born out of the work of the Holy Spirit in St. Paul Park with J. E. Forrest. Lewi Pethrus adopted the phrase in his campaign to plant churches throughout Sweden. This external focus outside of the existing church walls was a metric that organized the sending of the church. While the principle of sending the church does not change through the ages, the form that it takes may change. As most Swedish cities and towns all have one church within their city limits, other ideas must be drawn to begin churches in an order. Starting churches according to a contemporary metric of one church per ten thousand people would provide structure to plant.

The birth of the *Pingst* movement from the Holiness movement relied heavily on the leadership skills of Pethrus, Johnson, and Ongman. The structure of *Pingst* simply provided a form by which Holiness circles of prayer could congregate into larger groupings. As a homogenous culture, Sweden in the early 1900s displayed an entrepreneurial spirit, resulting in industrial developments, e.g., Nobel's dynamite, Karolinska Medical Institute, and Ericsson Telecommunications.[144]

Sweden also experienced revolutions in social grouping. Given the opportunities for new ideas in Swedish culture to take root, God's

---

143. Swedish—The promise will not disappoint.
144. Weibull, *Swedish History in Outline*, 118.

Spirit uniquely raised up believers who could recognize through implicit promptings of the Spirit to form *Pingst*. The idea that drove Pethrus et al. is that as the Holy Spirit is free to "blow where it wants," so the new conglomerate of churches is free to form and to propagate per the prompting of the Spirit.[145] The phrase "one church per city" contains Pethrus's understanding of the Holy Spirit's work in church planting strategy.

Of central focus to the writings of Pethrus and to the movement, certainly the primary expression that propelled the movement forward, can be found in the baptism in the Holy Spirit. Referenced previously in this section, *Helige Andes Dop*, was, in Pethrus's opinion, essential to the formation and sending of disciples: "No matter what is done with and to Christianity, no matter what revivals or spiritual movements may come, if the truth of the baptism of the Holy Spirit be left out, that revival or movement will never reach its intended goal."[146] In reference to the foundational experience of the baptism in the Holy Spirit found at the beginning of Acts 2, *Pingst* became known for their distinctive parallel praxis with the ancient church.

Summary

A theology and practicum of ecclesial outreach arose from the Spirit's leading, resulting in thousands of Swedes developing a vision of a redeemed Sweden. Assisting the formation of this denomination, Pethrus's leadership style was abrasive, challenging, decisive, and clear. The gathering point for new Pentecostal churches at the beginning of the twentieth century in Sweden occurred over the equipping power found in the baptism in the Holy Spirit. As a fifteen-year-old teenager, Pethrus took seriously his calling to change Sweden, Europe, and the world. The baptism in the Holy Spirit affected him, leading him to serve and send others throughout Sweden. While Pethrus's efficacy is difficult to match, his understanding of Pentecostal expression affected his sermon delivery as well as, at times, his abrasive leadership style. His legacy is known in the movement by the inspired idea of "one church per city."

CONCLUSION

The factors that affected *Pingst* as a church planting movement are couched in the perspective that God sent people through divine inspiration.

---

145. Wenell, *En Pentekostal Ecklesiologi*, 56.
146. Pethrus, *Wind Bloweth*, 22.

Early *Pingst* literature displays the baptism in the Holy Spirit in primary importance to accomplish the Disciple/Church Multiplication Cycle. Further, the Spirit-empowered leadership of Lewi Pethrus contributed to the creation of a denomination focused on the gospel of Jesus Christ. Within Sweden, *Pingst* originated as a collective of people who would organize their shared affinity for Spirit-empowered expressions of the cyclical process of church multiplication.[147] Where Jesus and Paul provided examples of how to engage others in disciple/church multiplication, *Pingst* attempted to continue this model through both practical and spiritual expression congruent to Scripture. The cyclical process of sending, proclaiming, gathering, and developing people to partake in *missio Dei* became a living process once the church experienced the baptism in the Holy Spirit, which Sweden had been waiting for.

How do current *Pingst* church planting pastors understand the activity of the Holy Spirit multiplication towards the unchurched? Among the influences upon their perception of this pneumatology, do they favor approaches found in Scripture, in historical concepts, or in contemporary sources?

---

147. Pingst, "Församlingsplantering—Pingst."

5

Field Research

THE SWEDISH CULTURAL CONTEXT includes a scientific materialism/naturalism coupled with dependence on the Swedish government. In the past, Pethrus and early church planters believed in the involvement of the Holy Spirit is essential to church planting. The biblical text demonstrates the power of the Holy Spirit as the catalyst and guide to making of disciples and proliferation of the church in the book of Acts. This study seeks to know the present day *Pingst* pastor's perception of the work of the Holy Spirit in church planting to discover if these cultural changes have influenced them.

METHODOLOGY

In researching the perspectives of humans, Q methodology developed by William Stephenson allows the subjectivity of one studied to arise in data.[1] Stephenson developed Q methodology by integrating (1) Sigmund Freud's pleasure principle and Charles Spearman's work on character, (2) ethical consideration, and (3) reality of the connection between mind and matter.[2] Q sort records one's spontaneous response to statements of behavior. Cognitively, opinions about each statement are then translated into the ordering of included statements onto a target grid to which parameters are assigned by the researcher.

---

1. Watts and Stenner, *Doing Q Methodological Research*, 25.
2. Stephenson, "Introduction to Q-Methodology," 3.

Research Design

Q sort is a unique research methodology which contributes to a holistic approach to researching a subject. To understand contemporary *Pingst* perceptions of pneumatology in church multiplication, a Q sort was employed, investigating both ideal and practiced perspectives. A brief interview follows the sorting, which provides a moment of reflection upon the most salient viewpoints. Interviews collected at the time of the Q sort, in addition to demographic questionnaires, supply data leading to greater accuracy in deriving the perspectives of Swedish *Pingst* pastors. Correlations also arise from the subjective data gathered from analyzing factors that represent these perspectives. Personal viewpoints can be discovered through the sorting process, yet the analysis of statistical data reveals the interrelated nature of the information. Demographic data analysis allows the researcher to understand currents and trends in ideals and practice, which may relate to age, experience, gender, and church planting context. The analysis and interpretation of the Q data is complete when both the researcher and the faculty adviser agree that the *Pingst* respondents' perceptions, as represented by their Q sorts.

Q Sort Concourse Construction

In constructing the concourse of statements, a Balanced Block design contains elements to envision three dimensions for each statement. Where three dimensions meet in the graphical depiction of twelve sub-cubes, there would need to be three representative statements that provide satisfactory representation.[3]

---

3. Bose, "Balanced Incomplete Block Designs," 619.no. 4 (1949

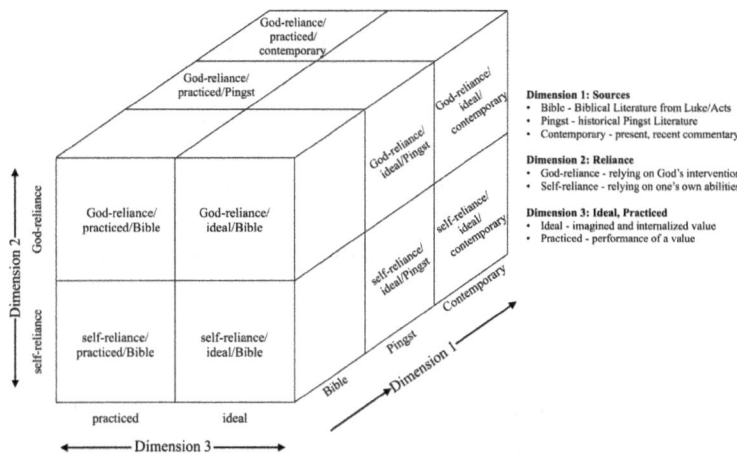

Fisher's Balanced Block Design

Dimension 1. Three Sources of Statements

The first dimension is found in the sourcing of statements that address the church planting process. Of the thirty-six statements, twelve are sourced from Lukan literature. These twelve are founded on scriptural verses that point to the Holy Spirit as the inspirator of explicit actions relating to church multiplication. Chapter 2 focuses on Lukan literature as a foundation of the Disciple/Church Multiplication Cycle, which lends to the credibility of the sourcing of these statements. The second set of twelve statements arise from *Pingst* archival literature representative of their foundational church planting movement in the early 1900s. The influence of Lewi Pethrus within *Pingst* is found in literature of correspondence and directive. Statements sourced from this material represents the pneumatology of early *Pingst* well. The third and final set of twelve statements are sourced from contemporary church planting efforts in Western contexts. Conferences and networks that focus solely on church planting have provided ideas and technology that attempt to engage communities in the disciple/church multiplication process.

Dimension 2. Reliance—God-Reliance, Self-Reliance

The second dimension is of reliance upon God or reliance upon humans to accomplish the work of God. This dimension reflects the positioning of the self by one's own efforts or through the effort of God. An implicit connection to the Holy Spirit may be understood to be the motivating force upon a person. Also, an explicit display of the activity of the Holy Spirit may be displayed. The presence in literature of addressing the Holy Spirit as a direct catalyst to church planting efforts will be considered as an indicator.

Dimension 3. Ideal, Practical

The third dimension considered is that which would be sorted by each respondent, the continuum of ideal vs practical. Ideal denotes an imaginative engagement with the best possible way that a *Pingst* church could form in Sweden. The actions of church planting are unearthed as the respondent provides information.

Participants

Q sort as a research instrument was chosen to unearth the behaviors, attitudes, and underlying perspectives of Swedish *Pingst* pastors. These pastors are grounded in their perspective primarily as believers in Christ, called to plant churches as Pentecostal pastors, and secondly, as participating citizens of Swedish culture.

The Pentecostal pastors who share in the research identify with the Christian denomination of *Pingst* where they work together in cooperation.[4] Currently, the denomination has no doctrinal tenets of faith in place. Their bonds are formally found in a contract that denotes proper behavior and rules of membership transfer between *Pingst* faith communities. Their self-identification as Pentecostals drives their cooperation. Further, they believe that their Spirit-empowered witness to the world is aligned with the theology of the Luke/Acts literature with focus on the experience and patterns found in Acts 2 regarding Spirit baptism.

Both elements of sociological homogeneity and diversity of Swedish people lends to forms of ideology that pervade culture in the form of cultural *grayness*.[5] This grayness allows for an increased efficacy in working with

---

4. Pingst, "Om Pingst—About Pingst."
5. Rojas, *Sweden after the Swedish Model*, 8.

human relationships where suspension of judgment is necessary.[6] Ordering of statements of importance and practice reveals hidden opinions that may be masked for the sake of inclusion of differing viewpoints.[7] A series of statements relating to my subject matter populate the research instrument.

Of the forty-four *Pingst* pastors who have participated in planting Pentecostal churches in Sweden within the last three years, thirty *Pingst* pastors took part in the research. Twenty-five of the respondents were male, and five were female (see Appendix A). All the participants are pastors as part of the *Pingst* network, which ordains its ministers through verification of copastors and leaders in close vicinity to them. All are fluent in Swedish with English as a second or third language. The municipalities where they have planted churches include small towns, small cities (15,000–49,000), medium cities (50,000–99,999), and large cities (100,000–150,000, suburban and urban). Each participant was asked to sort thirty-six different statements about church multiplication among the unchurched, from most to least importance according to their ideal perspective onto a target grid. Secondly, they were asked to sort the same statements from most to least practiced along the same target grid.

Procedure

To establish the ideal Pentecostal perspective, Q sort allows the subjectivity of each participant to become known. In comparing an initial ideal sort to a secondary practiced sort, an analyzation of convergence and divergence between the first and second sort must take place. The reasoning for researching the ideal and practiced perspectives of *Pingst* pastors provides opportunity for self-reflection about their goals and their present reality as well as consideration of the influence of their Pentecostal beliefs in the work of church multiplication. The instructions followed for each respondent can be found in Appendix D.

---

6. Elmer, *Cross-Cultural Servanthood*, loc. 155.
7. Bak, "Svenska Studenter Har Alla Svar."

98 The Spirit and the Secular

Personnel	Materials
• Interviewer (Phil)	• 36 statements re: church planting
• Respondent (Church Planter)	• Target grid to place statements

Sort #1: What is the ideal way
to plant a Pentecostal church?

Sort #2: What was your practiced way
to plant a Pentecostal church?

Question #1: Did the respondent notice differing
placement of statements between sorts?

Question #2: What did you learn through this exercise?

Interview Workflow

Q Sort 1

Respondents sorted the thirty-six statements onto a target grid which organized the responses from -4 to +4.

```
-4   -3   -2   -1   0   +1   +2   +3   +4
```

Target Grid for Thirty-Six Statements

This sort data was entered into the PQMethod computer program for analysis. A centroid factor extraction was performed, which computed a single relevant factor. Within this factor, the participants' responses were then flagged according to their shared perspective. Displaying these flagged perspectives on a scatterplot within PQMethod confirmed the unrotated factor. The creation of a robust representation of the ideal factor was followed by an analysis of the factor whereby PQMethod created a data file (.LIS) to display the statistical analysis (Appendix F). The factor indicated that twenty-four pastors possessed a shared understanding of what is the ideal way to plant Pentecostal churches in Sweden.

Q Sort 2

The second Q sort of the same thirty-six statements from Q sort 1 provides the perspective of what the Swedish Pentecostal pastor practices in the work of planting a church. This methodology follows the same procedure as the previous sort. PQMethod was used to analyze the information where two factors rose from the data. These were flagged for shared-values and then rotated to delineate the differing perspectives. To numerically delineate the differences between the perspectives, using the PQMethod software, Z scores were applied. Z scores display the distance between the mean average sort and a perspective. In researching thirty Pingst church planters about their perspectives of the activity of the Holy Spirit regarding church planting among the unchurched, utilization of Z scores in the descending array of differences provides perspective into their interrelationship (see Appendix G). For example, when considering statement 12 regarding offering education to church people about the gifts of the Holy Spirit, the set of Practical in Engagement holds a Z-score of .385 while Spiritual in Engagement holds a .854, a difference of -.469. This distance represents their difference in prioritization and value of the statement.

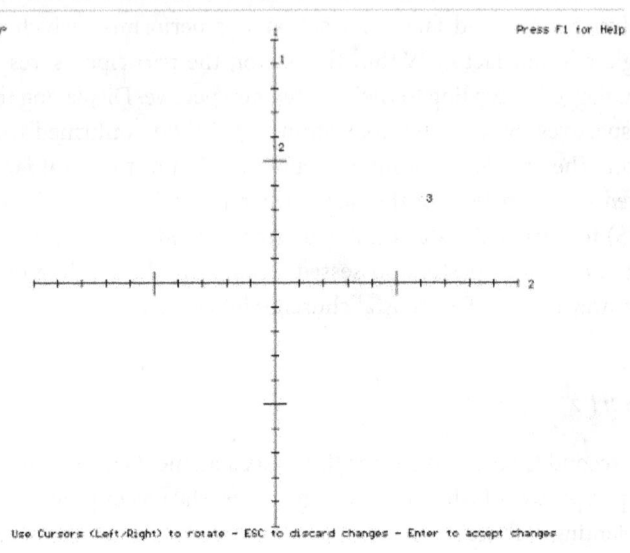

Scatterplot for Q Sort 2

Interviews within the framework of Q Sort

The Ideal sort of statements related to church planting was followed by two questions that inquired about their most intense responses found in the "+4" and "-4" columns of the target grid. To retain a clear sampling of each sort individually, no information was shared about the research instrument with the respondent prior to engaging in the research. The presence of the second sort was also retained until the conclusion of the first sort and interview.[8] The second sort of what was practiced followed suit as well through the inquiry about their responses. These reflections allowed the participants to realize the motives behind each sort.

Following the sorts and questions related to each individual sort, the respondent was asked about which statements they noticed had moved positions between the sorts from their perspective. This opportunity enabled the respondent to inquire and reflect themselves on parity and disparity between sorts in creating links within their own data with the assistance of the interviewer.[9]

8. Mitchell, *Secrecy and Fieldwork*, 13.
9. Fielding and Fielding, *Linking Data*, 47.

Follow-Up Question

The follow-up allows the respondent to notice the movement between sorts and allows the interviewer to review the entire process with the respondent in brief. After this, the researcher asks this question: "What did you learn from this experience of sorting/interview?"

PQMethod Computer Program

PQMethod is a statistical program that aids in computing Q sort methodology. One can enter, process, and analyze differing perspectives within this software. Relevant perspectives are flagged, chosen by the user to build a robust factor to compare to a secondary factor. The interrelation of these factors is then analyzed through PQMethod, generating a file which numerically provides this data. Interpretation of this data then leads to meaning being assigned by the user.

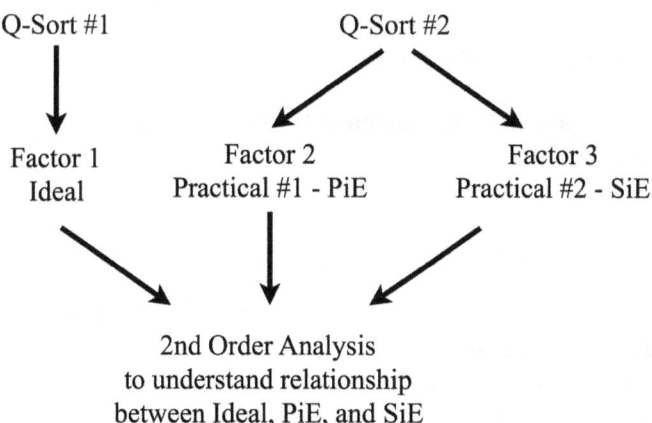

Q Sort/PQmethod Data Reduction

Informed Consent

Each interviewer received an explanation of interviewee rights. This consent was secured with each participant and included provision for their withdrawal from the study. A complete informed consent form was utilized.[10] The text used to inform the respondents can be found in Appendix D.

Based on the information gathered through the Q sort, the integrated interview and the demographic data of the Pentecostal pastors, what findings can be gleaned? What perceptions of the activity of the Holy Spirit have found a place in their thoughts and practices?

FINDINGS

As a result of the gathering of data through the Q sorts and brief qualitative interviews, categories of perspectives were derived from the field research.[11] As the Q sort presents the subjective realities of the respondents, the reflexive process involved in the integrated interview allows for observation of the self-education of the pastor.[12]

First Sort Findings: Description of Factors

This section presents a description of Factor 1 found from the second sort of statements.

Factor 1: Ideal or Balanced in Engagement

The factor array that details the inner workings of the Ideal sort represents the pinnacle of planting a Pentecostal church in Sweden. Prayer and fasting, the importance of the baptism in the Holy Spirit, mission, and securing relationship in a network of church planters are the common agreements depicting this sort. Baptizing people, finding a mother church, and prayer and fasting are the most agreed upon statements. A balanced approach to planting Pentecostal churches in Sweden characterizes this factor. An external mission focus, emphasis on spiritual empowerment, and pragmatic planning denote the top six agreed upon statements (see Table 5.1).

---

10. Sage, "Editor Guidelines."
11. McCracken, *Long Interview*, 16.
12. Lewis, *Missiological Research*, 16.

Table 5.1. Balanced in Engagement—Positive Responses

+3	+4
(6) Network with church planters[13]	(4) Mother church is a priority
(14) Baptism in the Holy Spirit	(26) Prayer and fasting
(29) Time with neighbors as mission	(27) Baptize and send in mission

Factor 1 can be summarized as those who share a balanced, networked, Pentecostal practice in mission. Participants who represent this sort value relationship with fellow believers, with God, and with their neighbors. In both +4 and +3, equal representation of mission, empowerment, and planning can be found. Conversely, they eschew interaction with those who favor public apologetics, volunteering at non-profit organizations, and the idea of equal care to everyone within the church.

Table 5.2. Balanced in Engagement—Negative Responses

-4	-3
(23) Informing about false teachers	(24) Holy Spirit only, no academics
(28) Sell all for others in need	(31) Equal care for all people
(35) Volunteer at non-profit organizations	(32) Secure a venue

Their praxis may be summarized as "Balanced in Engagement," as they focus with equal priorities on connection to God (upward), to fellow believers (inward), and to the unchurched (outward). The Ideal Factor provides equal directions of concern. Further, it values the Holy Spirit as the One who empowers and guides *Pingst* pastors in their church planting efforts. The Great Commission is also highly regarded in the Ideal in the sending of believers. What was not valued were those actions that historically may have been viable actions as found in the Bible and in the early days of church planting in the 1900s of Sweden, but which have been deemed to be not vital for today's church (see Table 5.2). Further, the Ideal sort also represents a pushback from Lewi Pethrus's statement that academic education is unnecessary, placing the statement in the most disagreed area of the grid.

---

13. Abbreviations of statements included here. Statements in entirety are found in Appendix B. "Networking" as a statement should be understood as self-reliance and not God-reliance.

In the area of neutrality, right in the middle of the sort, can be found two statements about church planting and obligation to the actions related to it. This indifference or gray area of neutrality reveals that contextualized approach to ministry as well as the obligation of church planting neither elicit strong agreement nor disagreement. The common factor that best represents the Ideal perspective among Swedish Pentecostal pastors who plant churches is that of being Balanced in Engagement. In practice, these pastors balance their direction in connecting to God, to fellow believers, and to the unchurched.

Second Sort Findings: Descriptions of Factors

This section presents a description of Factors 2 and 3 found from the second sort of statements.

Factor 2: Practical in Engagement

Factor 2 represents the bulk of those participating in the study. The twenty respondents who share in this perspective have a focus of practicality in the planting of a church. Statements that ranked high dealt with finding a mother church, networking with other church planters, as well as reading and explaining Scripture. Of statements that represent an explicit Pentecostal understanding, Baptism in the Holy Spirit and Prayer embodies the +3 and +4 ranges. Further, the +3 and +4 statements held the dimensions of Self-reliance balanced with God-reliance (50/50 percent). In another dimension of value, 86 percent of the statements were Practical, with 14 percent being Ideal. Half of these statements were sourced from the dimension of contemporary statements as opposed to the Bible or *Pingst* literature. Four statements matched the Ideal in high ranking: (1) networking with fellow church planters, (2) finding a mother church, (3) spending time with neighbors, and (4) baptism in the Holy Spirit. What distinguished Factor 2 from the Ideal is the focus on practical connections with people of similar life circumstance and contextualization. Their praxis can be summarized as "Practical in Engagement."

Table 5.3. Practical in Engagement—Positive Responses

+3	+4
(5) Reading and explaining Scripture	(4) Mother church is a priority
(14) Baptism in the Holy Spirit	(6) Network with church planters
(36) Pray alone and with others	(29) Time spent w/ neighbors

Factor 2 respondents started their church planting journey with a high value of idealism, feeling a need to ensure their church would survive the challenges of executing their plan. Practical systems took the place of the doctrinal, which shifted to +3. Further, the culture of church planting conferences and events that emphasize the practical aspect of planting a church can explain and assist this shift. Least practiced activities mirror the Ideal Factor 1 regarding false teachers, selling everything, volunteering, telling others about Christ's return, public evangelism, and integration with a municipal community.

Table 5.4. Practical in Engagement—Negative Responses

-4	-3
(23) Inform about false teachers	(22) Publicly evangelize
(28) Sell all for others in need	(24) Holy Spirit only, no academics
(35) Volunteer at non-profit organizations	(31) Equal care for all

Factor 3: Spiritual in Engagement

Factor 3 is characterized by an approach to church planting accentuated by prayer, mission, and the baptism in the Holy Spirit. The statements that ranked highest in the sort revealed the spiritual emphasis. According to the placement of the six most practiced statements amidst the Fisher diagram, the dimensions of Self-reliance and God-reliance were evenly distributed (50/50 percent), as were the Ideal and Practical representations. The Bible and *Pingst* literature contributed evenly (50/50 percent) to the statements, contributing to a semblance of completeness within the Factor 3 perception of their expression of Pentecostal Church Multiplication. Three statements from Factor 3 match the Ideal (Factor 1) in high ranking: seeking the baptism in the Holy Spirit, prayer and fasting, and baptizing/sending people in mission (see Table 5.5).

Table 5.5. Spiritual in Engagement—Positive Responses

+3	+4
(11) Testify about miracles	(14) Baptism in the Holy Spirit
(20) Praising God for his greatness	(26) Prayer and fasting
(22) Publicly evangelize	(27) Baptize and send people

Factor 3 (see Table 5.6) displayed a disregard for the influence of contemporary, practical actions such as technical production, social media, inspiration from successful church planters, and securing a venue, which all retained a low priority in practice of planting a church.

Table 5.6. Spiritual in Engagement—Negative Responses

-4	-3
(3) Inspiration from successful church planters	(23) Informing about false teachers
(9) Technical production	(24) Holy Spirit only, no academics
(13) Social media is a key component	(32) Secure a venue

Factor 3 can be best summarized in retaining their spiritual emphasis amidst practical challenges. By this characteristic, their praxis will be known as "Spiritual in Engagement" in that they strive to prioritize spiritual practices over practical.

Finding 1–1: From the *Pingst* Pastors Surveyed Regarding Church Planting, Three Factors Arise from the Q sort Process

These perspectives can be titled according to the characteristics: (1) Balanced in Engagement, (2) Practical in Engagement, and (3) Spiritual in Engagement. These three represent, in order, the ideal way to plant a Pentecostal church in Sweden, followed by two ways that are practiced in church planting. Within each perspective, connection to coworkers, to the unchurched, and to God are represented in the most valued statements.

Finding 1–2: The Baptism in the Holy Spirit is prioritized in the Ideal Set, PiE and SiE

What is similar across all factors is that they agree that the baptism in the Holy Spirit is a necessary practice in planting a Pentecostal church among the unchurched. The prioritization of seeking the baptism in the Holy Spirit is certainly emphasized in practice. In conjunction with this placement for a foundational Pentecostal principle, statements reflecting reliance on Holy Spirit follows the same pattern in the range of +2 to +4. Praying and Fasting, Baptizing and Sending, and Spending Time with Neighbors are highly regarded by all three factors.

Finding 1–3: Most Polarizing Statements were Rooted in Self-Reliance and Contemporary Thought

Polarizing statements are found by analyzing statements that display a difference in Z-score absolute value of +2 or above. These statements are in the following order from greatest difference: Networking (diff. 2.206), Public Evangelization (diff 2.199), Inspiration from Successful Church Planters (diff. 2.191), Selling Everything (diff. 2.164), Securing a Mother Church (diff. 1.737), Social Media (diff. 1.421), Volunteering at Compassion Organizations (diff. 1.310), and Allowing for Spontaneous Prayer (diff. 1.288). Six of the eight statements were found to be Contemporary as opposed to Bible/*Pingst* Literature. Five of the eight were sourced from situations of Self-reliance as opposed to God-Reliance.

Table 5.7. Most Polarizing Statements

Statements in order of intensity of polarization (greatest to least)	Z-Score (difference between factors)	Dimensions represented
Networking	2.206	Self-Reliance/Contemporary
Public Evangelization	2.199	Self-Reliance/Bible
Inspiration from successful Church Planters	2.191	Self-Reliance/Contemporary
Selling Everything	2.164	Self-Reliance/Pingst
Securing a Mother Church	1.737	Self-Reliance/Contemporary
Social Media	1.421	Self-Reliance/Contemporary
Volunteering at Compassion Organizations	1.310	God-Reliance/Contemporary
Allowing for Spontaneous Prayer	1.288	God-Reliance/Contemporary

Mixed Cases or "Lagom"

Present in the derivation of the practiced factors, a small sampling or respondents were found to group apart from the PiE and SiE. These respondents find themselves on the continuum between the two delineated factors. These perspectives belonged to neither Factor 2 nor 3, which will be addressed later in the description of the factors. In Q sort 2, twenty people represented Factor 2 while four people represented Factor 3. Six people represented a placement in-between the perspectives. Representation of varying city sizes as host contexts to the church plants was evenly spread throughout the factors. Factors 2, 3, and mixed all included small towns, medium sized cities, and both urban and suburban contexts. What stands out about this group as well is that all churches started by those interviewed are still open as lasting faith communities.

Table 5.8. Summary Descriptors of Factors

	Valued	Not Valued	Character Description
First Sort: FACTOR 1—Ideal Church Planting	-Mother church -Prayer and fasting -Networking -Baptism in the Holy Spirit -Baptizing and sending in mission -Engaging neighbors	-Securing a venue -No academia needed -Selling all -Teaching about false teachers -Volunteering in other orgs. -Equal care for all	Balanced in Engagement (BiE)
Second Sort: FACTOR 2— Practiced Church Planting	-Networking -Mother church -Engaging neighbors -Baptism in the Holy Spirit -Praying alone and w/ others -Reading and explaining scripture	-Publicly evangelize -Share about Christ's return -Teaching about false teachers -Selling all -Volunteering in other orgs.	Practical in Engagement (PiE)
Second Sort: FACTOR 3— Practiced Church Planting	-Testimonies about God -Baptism in the Holy Spirit -Baptizing and sending in mission -Publicly evangelizing -Praising God for his grace -Prayer and fasting	-Securing a venue -Teaching about false teachers -No academia -Gain inspiration from successful church planters -Social media -Technical production	Spiritual in Engagement (SiE)

This group will not be addressed further, yet the representation of an average practice of this study provides further information in perspective. Terminology found within Sweden gives a name for a way of thinking that does not lean toward extremes; "Lagom" or moderate summarizes this set.

Table 5.9. Demographic Profiles of Factors of Factor 2, Factor 3, and Mixed

	Factor 2 Practical in Engagement (20 respondents)	Factor 3 Spiritual in Engagement (4 respondents)	Mixed "Lagom" (6 respondents)
Average Age	42	43	42
% Female/Male	15/85	25/75	17/83
Married	100%	100%	100%
Believe in Baptism in the Holy Spirit as Subsequent to Salvation Yes-No	100%	100%	100%
Avg. Years in Ministry	18	22	19
Avg. Education	35% Gymnasiet[1] 0% Examen[2] 25% Masters	25% Gymnasiet 75% Examen	16% Gymnasiet 33% Examen 50% Masters
Context Most Rep.	Small-Medium cities	Urban	Suburban
Status of Church Planted	80% open	75% open	100% open

1. High school.
2. Bachelor's degree.

Q SORT SECOND-ORDER ANALYSIS OF FACTOR 1, FACTOR 2, FACTOR 3

To make sure that this study is comparing the outputs of two separate analyses fairly, these outputs of Q sort 1 and Q sort 2 placed as input into a new second-order analysis for the specific purpose of direct comparison. BiE, PiE and SiE were found through the process of data reduction via factor analysis, resulting in representative factor arrays, which could then be placed on a target grid for clear perspective. To suit the purpose of the second-order analysis of the data, the representative sorts of BiE, PiE, and SiE that emerged from the previous separate sorting tasks gathered. Data processed through flagging and rotation produces a resulting data file for perspective in how both PiE and SiE measured against the Ideal Factor, BiE (see Appendix G).

In interpreting the data file for the second-order analysis, attention must be paid to the loadings of the perspectives found between the factors (see Table 5.10). PiE (Factor 2) displayed a deep similarity to the Ideal (Factor 1). In considering the two practiced perspectives, the greatest amount of drift from the Ideal is SiE, who allow explicitly Pentecostal statements to be favorable in place of practical statements. In the SiE, Public Evangelism replaced Reaching out to Neighbors and Praising God replaced Securing a Mother Church. By these results, PiE is closer to the Ideal than SiE.

Table 5.10. Second-Order Analysis Factor Matrix with Loadings Represented (X Represents Flagged Loadings)

	Factor 1	Factor 2
BiE	0.9254X	0.0018
PiE	0.5628X	-0.0040
SiE	0.3551	0.6033X

Finding 1–4: PiE and SiE Self-Identify as Pentecostals. The Stress of Planting a Church Propels Their Implicit Notions of Pentecost into Explicit Action.

To be clear, there is no test of the acumen of one's Pentecostal convictions and nature. Since all pastors in this study have decided to express that they have received the baptism in the Holy Spirit and have subscribed to the idea of subsequence to salvation, they have found a place in *Pingst*. Their expressions of planting a church to the unchurched vary yet fall along the aforementioned Factors 2 and 3. Investigating the data further, the motif of church planting within the statements ranks higher for PiE than SiE. As their Practical in Engagement label suggests, Factor 2 tends towards acts of service outward in connection to others.

Finding 1–5: Both Factor 2 (PiE) and 3 (SiE) Expressed a Desire to Alter Their Practice and Return to the Ideal, Balanced in Engagement.

As a part of the Q sort process, two final questions were offered to the respondents. First, they were asked which statements between Q sort 1 and Q sort 2 did they recognize had moved. After each respondent pointed out the statement that had moved, they then expressed their own thought about the movement between sorts (see Table 5.11).

Table 5.11. Self-Recognized Movement between Q Sort 1, Ideal and Q Sort 2, Practiced (Statements Listed in Order of Highest Movement to Least)

	Practical in Engagement PiE	+/- grid spots moved	Spiritual in Engagement SiE	+/- grid spots moved
Higher quantity of recognition	32. Securing a venue	+4	28. Selling possessions and give away to all	+5
	9. Tech production	+3	22. Publicly evangelizing	+5
	13. Social media	+3	3. Inspiration from successful church planters	-5
	26. Prayer and fasting	-2	6. Networking with other church planters	-5
^ | | | | v	15. Sending people in mission to other towns	-2	4. Securing a mother church	-4
			13. Social media	-3
			19. Allowing for spontaneous prayer	+3
Lower quantity of recognition			35. Volunteer at compassion organizations	+3

These responses provide a collective recognition of the movement. Table 5.11 shows that Factors 2 and 3 recognized that their Q sort 2 was not in parity with the ideal sort and expressed a desire for right praxis.

Responses to PiE Movement

After recognizing the movement, the interviews delivered pointed observations.

On Social Media, Technical Production and Venue

13. "People actually look at what is going on in the church before visiting." (PP-13, 2)
13. "We placed so much hope in this (Social Media)." (PP-06, 1)
13. "What is interesting to me is how high social media climbed." (PP-25, 2)
9. "This moved drastically because we had a high focus on production and influences from other church planters." (PP-06,1)
9. "We realized that Technical and Venue are somehow connected." (PP-17, 2).
32. "Venue was necessary to the group. Practicality took over." (PP-12, 2)
32. "Venue is up there because we needed a place to meet. We have moved from homes, to pubs, to clubs. When we studied the movement in the past, *Pingst* people always looked for a place to meet in the center of town. This was a priority." (PP-07, 2)

On Suffering

16. "We don't have a great amount of suffering. As adults, we don't suffer here." (PP-23, 2)
16. "Ideally, we need more boxes because paying the price is important, practically. This, 100 percent determines the outcome of the church plant. We didn't talk about this much at the beginning, but we practiced this." (PP-28, 2)

On Prayer and Fasting

26. "This had to be higher on the chart in the future." (PP-11, 2)
26. "We don't want to be legalistic in praying and fasting." (PP-27, 2)

Field Research

On the Baptism in the Holy Spirit and Prophetic Words

> 14. "We want to practice this more, hopefully that is clearer as we move forward. Even though this is what we want for the church we need to be clearer about this in the future." (PP-17, 2)
> 8. "Prophetic words helped us against all odds." (PP-26, 2)
> 8. "The prophetic has been more important than we initially thought. Coming back to the prophetic helps us to focus. We need to hear from God first to plant a church." (PP-07, 2)

On Eschatology and Mission

> 10. "Thinking about this a bit more as Jesus *is* the Savior, the world's hope . . . We want people to come to faith. This should be higher up in my placement." (PP-15, 2)
> 15. "We are trying to start a church that starts churches." (PP-22, 2)

Responses to SiE Movement

After recognizing the movement between the sorts, those interviewed responded with their own remarks.

On Selling Everything and Giving the Proceeds to Others in Need

> 28. "Spending time in church planting is an investment that will cost everything." (PP-18, 2)
> 28. "We did sell everything and gave it all away in the beginning. This was a good start." (PP-14, 2)

On Public Evangelism

> 29. "Public evangelization must not compete with us reaching our neighbor. Neighbors are right there." (PP-18, 2)
> 22. "We thought public street ministry would save our city early on, and we still do. Yet, there is nothing like winning your neighbors for Christ." (PP-14, 2)

On the Baptism in the Holy Spirit and Miracles

> 14. "Baptism in the Holy Spirit became so important." (PP-19, 1)
> 11. "Miracles play a big part in people coming to faith. My real situation changed this." (PP-19, 2)

On Eschatology and Mission

> 11. "It is important to let people know that Jesus is coming back. This has to do with if a person can have peace with God today, or not." (PP-18, 2)
> 13. "We need to focus on friends, family, and workmates, not on social media." (PP-19, 2)

DISCUSSION

After an analysis of the Q sort data, the most important findings are found in the categorization and contrast of dissimilarity between the factors. The grouping of the factors per the characteristics of those statements most valued provides clarity on the singular ideal that the church planters hold to be of importance. Just as well, the practiced perspectives of the church planters reveal the understanding of the pastors on the involvement of the Holy Spirit.

Research Questions Answered

This study researched three major questions: (1) What ideal viewpoints of the activity of the Holy Spirit as related to church planting among the unchurched are represented in contemporary *Pingst* pastor's perceptions? (2) What did the practiced viewpoints reveal about their perceptions? and (3) What correlations can be drawn from the comparison of the results of the research instrument? The answer to the first question is found in an analysis of Q sort 1.

Factor 1, which became known as Balanced in Engagement, or BiE, revealed the importance of prayer and fasting and of trusting the Holy Spirit to provide guidance. Also, baptism in the Holy Spirit ranked highly in this sort, showing that this distinctive would have a place in the ideal planting of a Pentecostal church towards the unchurched. Mission and baptism are found as components of the top statements, which are represented as well, emphasizing the baptism in the Holy Spirit to those interviewed. The Disciple/Church Development Cycle is present in the ranking of these statements. The BiE sort displayed an integrated approach to being Pentecostal pastors who are planting churches with a focus toward reaching the unchurched. This integration is understood by recognizing the empowerment of people, their passion to reach the unchurched, and their gaining of support to accomplish the task in making disciples and planting new churches.

On Identification as Pentecostals

The second research question was answered as Practical in Engagement (PiE) and Spiritual in Engagement (SiE), which were revealed through analysis of their groupings through Q sort 2. All pastors involved in this study have self-identified as Pentecostals, yet the working out of their theologies differ. The PiE group placed statements of self-effort and contemporary sourcing at a high ranking in comparison to the Ideal. This placement made known that their practice of prayer and mission lessened in importance. Their implicit trust in the Holy Spirit to guide them in other areas of priority as they identify as Pentecostal pastors who have received the baptism in the Holy Spirit. A great deal of their perspective pays attention to the context surrounding them.

SiE ranked statements highly, which focused on explicit expressions of the Holy Spirit's influence, testimonies of miracles, prayer, and the Great Commission. In church planting situations, their center of activity would be in seeking guidance from the Holy Spirit regardless of the context. SiE respondents source their statements of importance from the Bible, overlapping with *Pingst* practices from earlier literature about church planting. Across all three perspectives, BiE, PiE, and SiE, the Pentecostal distinctive of the baptism in the Holy Spirit was valued as a top priority.

PiE would find their Pentecostal identity as best represented in their high ranking of Networking and Securing a Mother Church. As their work in church planting is rooted in self-effort and contemporary sources, they hold to a core of Christian traits that they do not doubt that they possess. Also, their expectation of being Pentecostal is clear in their ideal way of sorting. They point to biblical examples where congregations of Spirit-empowered believers exist, and hierarchy to help the common vision forward. They would rely on their Swedish cultural propensity to be a part of an interactive whole community for survival as individual practitioners.

Some statements from Factor 2 reveal their own Pentecostal underpinnings: "God spoke in an audible voice to me while I was speaking in tongues" (PP-26, 1). "I am praying, and the full will of God goes beyond my intellectual capacity" (PP-23, 1). "We live in the Holy Spirit as a church" (PP-15, 1). "The baptism in the Holy Spirit is important to have power. To reach people and be led to them" (PP-07, 1).

SiE includes those who find their Pentecostal identity in reliving the experiences they have been informed of from the Bible and *Pingst* literature. Their expression of being a Spirit-empowered believer is rooted in signs and wonders, prayer, and the manifestation of the gifts of the Holy Spirit. Their expectation of the Pentecostal experience is that of a self-edification and of evangelism. They believe, yet they need to be reminded of the Pentecostal catalyst that sent them into times of prayer and mission.

On Baptism in the Holy Spirit

Factors 1–3 highly valued the Baptism in the Holy Spirit, no matter the ideal or practice of the church planter. Of the six most important statements in the sorts, two statements were found to be similar between Ideal and PiE, and Ideal and SiE, respectively. Ideal and PiE shared the practical based statements of Networking and Securing a Mother Church. Ideal and SiE shared spiritual statements of Prayer and Fasting and Baptizing and Sending People. As the respondents agree on an ideal way of planting, their practices are different in emphasis.

In sorting Q sort 1 to establish the ideal, those who became a part of PiE also sorted the baptism in the Holy Spirit to a high ranking. "We need the Baptism in the Holy Spirit in order to accomplish what he (God) wants" (PP-05, 1). "The Baptism in the Holy Spirit provides our power to share the gospel. We need to be filled and inspired by this" (PP-10, 1). "This is the foundation to our faith" (PP-17, 1). "This fuels our ministry" (PP-20, 1). "The Baptism in the Holy Spirit is the key, it's biblical" (PP-26, 1). The representative conviction in ideal and practice is that the baptism in the Holy Spirit is important to starting a church. In practice, however, practical statements reflecting self-effort rank higher than in the initial sort.

Further, participants grouped into SiE regarding practice noted the importance of the baptism in the Holy Spirit. "The Spirit's leading is the fire for ministry in my life" (PP-19, 1). "I don't think it's possible to raise the dead or walk on water without the baptism in the Holy Spirit. We need to be clothed in the same power as he (Jesus) was" (PP-14, 1). "This is what keeps me in ministry" (PP-01, 1). Baptism in the Holy Spirit was placed in the highest ranking in this factor.

The baptism in the Holy Spirit prompts the transformation of a believer into a servant to fulfill these expressions. Luke's treatment of the Holy Spirit never provides a case that the Spirit is the direct cause for someone to decide to "orient one's life towards God."[14] Luke does, however, cite the influence of the Spirit prior to an act of service or spiritual expression akin to the higher rankings of SiE. By this, one can further understand that the equipping of the Spirit is for all believers to serve as witnesses. In Sweden in the action of church planting among the unchurched arises in Factors 2 and 3. Both PiE and SiE fully expect to recognize and function as Spirit-empowered witnesses, thereby Pentecostal.

Polarizing Statements / Implicit Notion to Explicit Action

Polarizing statements from the Q sort reveal the internal convictions of the pastors. Z-scores assigned to the statements presented a difference between the perspectives of PiE and SiE. In Table 8, categories of these statements can be derived.

Conference-Centered Church Planting

Networking, inspiration from successful church planters, securing a Mother Church, and social media are of value to the PiE church planter. Spending time in organized church planting conferences, get-togethers, books, podcasts, and social media is of high value. Internal security within the grouping of church planters matters to this group. Being a good steward of the material of a church plant is of high value. Their implicit understanding of survival of the church plant is rooted in their understanding of work of the Holy Spirit in calling and seeing their work as the work of the Spirit. Networking together with others occurs at gatherings rallying around church planting, with successful church planters as examples. PiE approaches the act of church planting with pragmatism.

Ministry-Centered Church Planting

Public evangelization, selling everything, volunteering at compassion organizations, and allowing for spontaneous prayer are of high value to

14. Menzies, *Empowered for Witness*, 144.

an SiE church planter. Their emphasis on explicit expressions of the Holy Spirit in speech, service, and prayer is not shared by their PiE counterparts. The action of planting a church is found in the embodiment of working out God's direction in proclaiming the gospel outwardly, by valuing life spent with others, yet not focusing on the center of a church plant as originating from a conference. They may hear from God and then simply perform that action that they feel the Holy Spirit is impressing upon them quite fluidly.

While the PiE utilize practical means to establish security for the survival of the church plant through their trust of the Holy Spirit in relationship to other church planters, SiE rely on actions, which places hope in the survival of the church plant through their understanding of the Holy Spirit as involved in ministry to people.

Returning to the Ideal

The third research question was answered through the investigations of findings for correlations between parity and disparity between the perspectives. Difference regarding the importance of practical and spiritual statements displayed how church planting efforts range across a spectrum of interpretations of what it means to be Pentecostal. Their responses, rooted in practical and spiritual awareness, were open to correction by revelation of their perspectives through the research instrument. There was a sense of concern in the expressions of the practiced efforts of both the PiE and SiE, who all hoped to return to the ideal, BiE, after reflecting on their past work. By their comments, the future values that they all hoped to have would seek to realize the ideal in their own practice.

Ideal Values / Q-Sort 1	Practiced Values / Q-Sort 2	Future Values / Interview
"Balanced in Engagement" (Ideal)	66% of pastors - "Practical in Engagement" (Practiced perspective 1)	"Balanced in Engagement" (Ideal)
	20% of pastors - Mixed, "*Lagom*"	
The majority of pastors sorted to adhere to the same ideal in planting a Pentecostal church	13% of pastors - "Spiritual in Engagement" (Practiced perspective 2)	100% of pastors expressed regret, hoping to return to the ideal
	The majority of pastors favored practical engagement as opposed to spiritual engagement	

Ideal, Practiced, and Future Values

The balance as found in the ideal sort is the dynamic perspective generated through the Q sort methodology, which can change in future sorts.

A noted desire to return to the ideal can be seen in their comments on what they learned from the research tool. In considering the scatterplot of the loadings, PiE or Factor 2 is closer to the ideal, Factor 1. SiE, Factor 3, may have a longer journey to establish parity with their ideal of how a Pentecostal church are planted among the unchurched.

> "All of these statements provide light on what is a priority. I am thinking about if I was to start a church again, what should I focus on this next time." (PP-18,2)
>
> "The greatest thing I learned is that the model I think of and real life are different." (PP-19, 2)
>
> "This reveals my heart and mind. It reveals how I think and helps me to evaluate what I think and do." (PP-21, 2)
>
> "This tool would be good to practice once a year to stay on course." (PP-24, 2)
>
> "To plant a Pentecostal church, 70 percent of these statements need to be in place. We have to set our priorities and stick to our priorities." (PP-03, 2)
>
> "We are in a journey back to the spiritual from our practical focus. We depended much on the practical in our efforts. I wanted to stack the middle! This challenges me to see what I think is important now in comparison to what we did." (PP-04, 2)
>
> "This would be a good exercise for a team to do . . . to reflect on what we do and why we do it. I think all of these statements will be important in different contexts within Sweden." (PP-29, 2)
>
> "We need to refocus on prayer, this is important." (PP-05, 2)
>
> "This was a good exercise and challenge for church planters. For a multi-campus church to do this would be good." (PP-26, 2)
>
> "Through the exercise I'm visualizing the fact that there has been a great amount of change in 12 years of church planting. I hope it shows maturity; it certainly is experience." (PP-09, 2)
>
> "We can be so focused on the next service or small group that we may miss out on that moment to practice a spiritual discipline." (PP-10, 2)
>
> "My Ideal and Practiced diverged from one another. Some of my answers I would have liked to have ranked higher." (PP-11, 2)
>
> "Some things can certainly be redone so that they are closer to the ideal." (PP-15, 2)
>
> "I would like to stop a bit more and think about what I'm doing and why I'm doing it. The problem is that I'm running. I need to take a moment and organize my priorities." (PP-16, 2)
>
> "How we do things in the right and wrong way are revealed. This helps me to reflect on the future." (PP-22, 2)

"We need to be sure about that we do what we set out to do. Theory and reality don't always meet. This shows me how importance and practice are separate in some areas. This is a good tool for reflection." (PP-27, 2)

In review of the differing perspectives, reconciliation of the drift from the ideal may provide greater results according to the pastors involved. While the desire to return to the ideal is evident in every interview that followed the Q sort process, I believe it highly unlikely that a church planter could match their practice entirely with their ideal. Striving after this parity assists a shared, imaginative form of the Pentecostal church forward into the future.

Considering the cultural lens of Swedish people, their identity as Swedes will only provide strength to their pursuits to returning to a place of theory and practice that is balanced, *Lagom*.

CONCLUSION

This study demonstrates how *Pingst* pastors experience a divergence between their theology or theory and praxis when church planting. Further, once recognizing this divergence through a change agent, they are aware of this disparity. Accountability and desire for right practice are revealed as core traits of these *Pingst* pastors.

Of the thirty *Pingst* pastors who took part in the research, each one was thankful for the opportunity to rethink their current church planting practices. The identity of *Pingst* pastors is found in their shared experience of the baptism in the Holy Spirit as a catalyst for service, as well as in their relational non-profit organization in Sweden. How each pastor expresses perspectives throughout the church planting process can emphasize or deemphasize the spiritual or the practical.

For transformation towards a balanced Spirit-led church planting theology to occur, longitudinal adjustments by *Pingst* pastors to their ideal seems to be in their best interest as a movement. Sources for the statements reflect the influences that pastors can allow to assist them in their efforts. This study discovered the pastors' perspectives of the activity of the Holy Spirit regarding church planting among the unchurched in contemporary Swedish Pentecostal church planting. Three different approaches display how their identity as *Pingst* pastors is worked out implicitly and explicitly. Based on a biblical, historical, and cultural understanding that informs the reader of the respondents' ideals and practiced perceptions, what theory can be synthesized to effectively assist in future church planting efforts among the unchurched?

6

A Theory of Pentecostal Church Multiplication among the Unchurched

THIS STUDY REVIEWED PERSPECTIVES of the activity of the Holy Spirit in church multiplication among the unchurched. It examined the interaction of the Holy Spirit in the proclaiming, gathering, developing, and sending of disciples. Further, this research investigated the parallel strategy of Jesus and Paul as found in Lukan literature, both making disciples within their context through the power and guidance of the Holy Spirit. In addition, reviews of the cultural context, historical ecclesial literature, and contemporary pastoral perspectives provided information about the unchurched Swedish perspectives of pneumatological activity. In examining the multiple perspectives represented, divine interaction and guidance is imperative to church multiplication efforts.

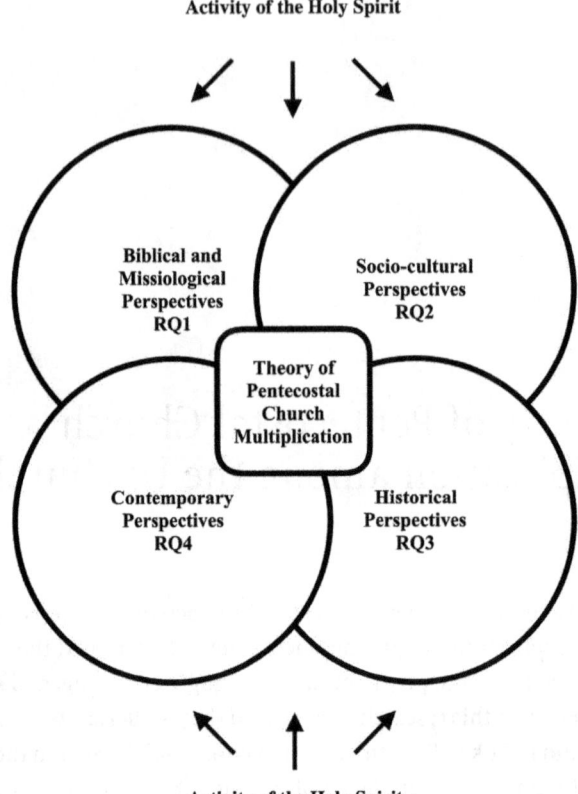

Integration of Perspectives Informs a Theory of Pentecostal Church Multiplication

As *Pingst* pastors engage in reviewing the process of church multiplication, they exhibit an awareness of their shared ideal in contrast to their practiced methods of ministry. Their cultural challenge includes engaging an increasingly secular and pluralistic context with the gospel of Jesus Christ. Honoring the biblical within the context of early *Pingst* examples of making disciples challenges pastors to retain fidelity to Scripture as well as to innovate ministry forms as Lewi Pethrus did to plant churches. Evaluation of this research leads to this question: How should a *Pingst* pastor go about planting Pentecostal churches in Sweden? This chapter will combine the outcomes gleaned from the biblical/missiological, sociocultural, historical *Pingst*, and field research to develop a theory of Pentecostal church multiplication among the unchurched of Sweden.

A Theory of Pentecostal Church Multiplication among the Unchurched 125

OVERVIEW OF BIBLICAL/MISSIOLOGICAL AND EARLY PINGST RESEARCH

This research investigated Scripture, missiological sources, and early *Pingst* literature to identify explicit activity of the Holy Spirit in the process of church multiplication. In reviewing the segments utilized by Luke in his writing of his Gospel and the book of Acts, the ministry of Jesus and Paul revealed a Cycle of Disciple/Church Multiplication containing the stages of sending, proclaiming, gathering, and developing. The Holy Spirit was the catalyst for the inspiration and motivation of the disciples into each successive phase of the process. As Jesus encouraged the apostles to wait for the baptism by the Holy Spirit as part of the development phase of the cycle, both the early church and Paul would follow his example.

Reliance upon the Holy Spirit for guidance in the mobilization of the church is categorized in the sending portion of this process. Proclamation is attributed to the examples of Spirit-inspired speech by Jesus and his disciples in sharing about God's Kingdom. Examples of gathering are found in the early church (Acts 1, 2, 16). Early *Pingst* literature revealed a collection similar to biblical occurrences of the cycle. Swedes attracted to God through the Holiness movement and other charismatic groupings sought God and were baptized in the Holy Spirit, akin, but not exclusively connected to the development phase. As people became empowered, they were then sent by a phrase attributed to the spiritual imagination of Lewi Pethrus, "one church per city," which guided much of the sending efforts of *Pingst*. Each faith community produced through the sending of missionaries into Sweden would culminate in the gathering of believers and non-believers to witness the gospel of Jesus Christ as a crucial point of the church. These churches would house opportunities for Swedes to be developed into Spirit-empowered believers who would be sent to continue the cycle.

OVERVIEW OF FIELD RESEARCH AND SOCIOCULTURAL RESEARCH

The *Pingst* church planters interviewed collectively expressed an ideal perspective in what it means to be Pentecostal in the cycle of disciple/church multiplication. Many of these pastors have grown up in the church and received a call to ministry by God. Along with pastoring believers, the *Pingst* denomination had challenged them to reach the unchurched in their communities. Fueled by the baptism in the Holy Spirit, church planting is an opportunity to form a more culturally congruent approach to engaging society with the gospel.

The foundational perception of Swedish Secular Humanists diminishes the significance of the activity of the Holy Spirit. To engage the humanist mindset, many of the attempts to capture the attention of the unchurched have relied on practices based in practical statements of church multiplication. The Practical in Engagement perspective maintained an implicit Pentecostal stance in church multiplication, reliance in networking with colleagues, and following successful examples of church planting for inspiration.

Conversely, the Spiritual in Engagement perspective relied on practices which emphasized spiritual practices in church multiplication. Their understanding was that Spirit-empowerment is to be explicit in one's ministry expressions of church planting towards the unchurched. Prayer and fasting as well as the baptism in the Holy Spirit are common practice for their perspective in planting a church.

When reviewing their own efforts in consideration of a shared ideal viewpoint of what it is to plant a Pentecostal church, both Practical in Engagement and Spiritual in Engagement expressed *regret* towards their practices. The heuristic experience of the reflection tool provided inspiration to include spiritual practices in tandem with the practical in both PiE and SiE perspectives. They aspire to become more like the Ideal, Balanced in Engagement. Key to forming a theory, their interviews revealed a desire to exhibit an equilibrium in church multiplication statements that relate to coworkers, the unchurched, and to God (inward, outward, and upward). Their perspectives found that to be a Swedish Pentecostal pastor who plants churches among the unreached is to maintain an interrelated nature with the Spirit to minister effectively.

A THEORY OF PENTECOSTAL CHURCH MULTIPLICATION FOR UNCHURCHED IN SWEDEN

The Holy Spirit provides inspiration and guidance for contemporary *Pingst* church planters. Their shared ideal perspective in how to plant a Pentecostal church as Spirit-empowered. As revealed through this research, *Pingst* church multiplications practices can drift from their ideal. This can lead to churches that are practical cultural interpretations of the planter, in tension with attempts to retain Christ as the center of the church.

Also revealed in the field research, contemporary *Pingst* pastors share in the perspective that church multiplication activities are not possible apart from the baptism in the Holy Spirit occupying the highest point of salience in practice. This similar understanding speaks not of the dogma of *Pingst* as the heart and soul of the movement but of God's Spirit at work in humankind so that Christ is known to the unchurched. The results of the field research disclose a desire to have balance in relational directions and in implicit/explicit activity of the Holy Spirit. The BiE perspective may provide the best present perspective by which to multiply Spirit-empowered disciples and churches.

The Cycle of Disciple/Church Multiplication provides a framework by which to hang a theory of Pentecostal church multiplication among the unchurched in Sweden. A Spirit-empowered, balanced approach would provide relevant values to sending, proclaiming, gathering, and developing disciples. Further, the usage of the term *Pingst* as the name of the denomination confirms a theological direction that finds efficacy in ministry through Spirit-empowerment. Findings reveal consistency in *Pingst* pastors' expressions of desired Pentecostal-ness, regardless of perspective. As this model is utilized, *Pingst* pastors can retain a course of ministry that finds a balance in valuing working as a faith community (inward), reaching neighbors (outward), and living as a disciple in connection to God (upward).

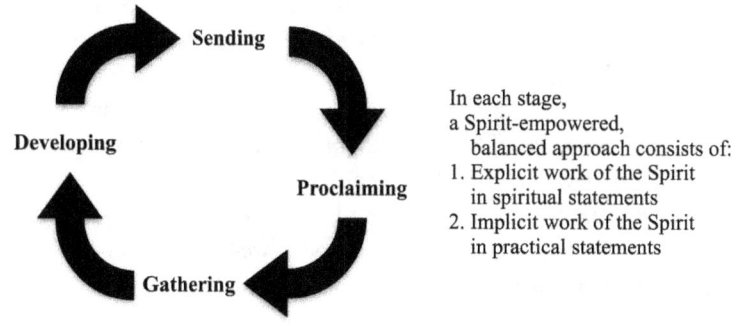

Spirit-Empowered, Balanced Approach to Planting Swedish Pentecostal Churches

Balance, then, would also address the synthesis of both practical and spiritual statements contributing to each stage of the cycle. Implementation of a Spirit-empowered, balanced approach would consist of representation of both (1) the explicit work of the Spirit as found in spiritual statements and (2) the implicit work of the Spirit as found in practical statements. Revisiting the field research instrument as a tool to realign to an ideal will serve to lessen gaps found between theory and praxis. This section will underpin this theory by showing that a Spirit-empowered, balanced engagement in the process of church multiplication will assist *Pingst* pastors in reaching the unchurched.

Sending

This study found that sending is one of four key principles in the Cycle of Disciple/Church Multiplication, which can benefit from a Spirit-empowered, balanced approach. Sending denotes the mobilization of disciples to take part in engaging the unchurched established by Jesus and maintained by Paul (Luke 9:1–6; 10:1–23; 13:1–3). The baptism in the Holy Spirit of Acts 2 catalyzed the sending of the disciples towards those who would hear the gospel of Jesus Christ.[1] The assembly of believers then, in conjunction with the leading of the Holy Spirit, would commission those to be sent.

Spirit-empowerment compels the church to look outside of their current structure to engage those who have not heard and understood the gospel of Jesus Christ. This sending motion of the church is integral to the multiplication of churches as it releases believers to proclaim the gospel in contexts where the gospel currently has no meaning. The secular climate of Sweden has been engaged with the gospel throughout history in varying situations and venues. However, generations of Swedes have not heard and understood the gospel yet have been exposed to liberal Christian theology, which has diluted the meaning of Jesus's message so that it fits into an acceptable pantheon of Swedish pluralism. Lewi Pethrus's desire to plant churches "one church per city" provided a vision to fulfill for the *Pingst* disciples. The city that would have a church planted would be the metric by which to gauge their progress. The commissioning of missionaries to be sent to share the gospel in cities without a Pentecostal church led to the proliferation of new churches throughout Sweden.

Pastors must trust that being sent to the unchurched requires Spirit-empowerment that requires devotion to God as well as practical application. Realizing this dynamism within Pentecostal church multiplication efforts will assist in reaching those both near and far for Christ.

Proclaiming

The Cycle of Disciple/Church Multiplication also contains the act of proclaiming. Under one's own power, the propensity to divulge affiliation with Christ, as in the case of Peter, may be fraught with doubt and disloyalty (Luke 22:54–62). After waiting on the baptism of the Holy Spirit, however, the response of the apostles to accusations by the surrounding crowd elicited a response characterized by bravery and conviction (Acts 2). Aside from this display, Peter's speech, inspired by the Holy Spirit, shared the

---

1. Coleman and Graham, *Master Plan of Evangelism*, loc. 722.

gospel to the Jewish people with contextual precision, creating meaning in their hearts. Peter and the apostles shared their Spirit-empowered message in those places designated by Jesus Christ—simultaneously in Jerusalem, Judea, Samaria, and the ends of the Earth (Matt 28:18–20).

Upon realizing that he had been baptized in the Holy Spirit, Lewi Pethrus purposed the *Pingst* church to share the message with all of Sweden. His roots as a Baptist contributed to his knowledge of the Bible, yet his Pentecostal experience propelled him in establishing written proclamations of the gospel, publishing them as a series, which would be bound as a book and then sent along with itinerant preachers. Many Swedes heard the gospel in the early 1900s through the Spirit-empowered proclamation of Pethrus and other Pentecostals. Numerically, Pethrus was the most successful church multiplier in all of Sweden. He started churches in urban settings and then sent preachers to smaller cities to establish not only the presence of Spirit-empowered preachers among the unchurched but organized preaching outposts as well. The spiritual fervor and activity of the Holy Spirit surrounding their efforts of proclamation captured the attention of many people, resulting in the multiplication of disciples. Speaking in tongues, prophetic words, and prayer for healing earmarked *Pingst* ministerial work at that time.

Ninety years later, the cities where *Pingst* churches were planted have grown in population and in secularity. Contemporary Sweden's culture of secular humanism does not identify explicit pneumatological activity as notable. This can mean that speaking in tongues or prophecy may be recognized yet disregarded. The Holy Spirit does not only work explicitly but can also create relationship with the unchurched through his implicit guidance. Through interaction with a Spirit-empowered believer, a Swede may recognize the encounter as potentially divine, which would challenge their worldview. Within a sociological grouping of Swedish people who gather around a subject of shared affinity,[2] there exists opportunity to exchange ideas. This affinity group is the new forum to transform the unchurched. Creation of these opportunities to walk alongside the unchurched in close proximity can provide a favorable moment of engagement. This method of proclamation also denotes a sociologically welcoming environment of the church.

Further, as the unchurched are historically unlikely to enter Pentecostal worship spaces in Sweden, perception of the Holy Spirit in outreach may begin with reimagining the space of the faith community, lending to the overwhelming amount of practical considerations found in the field research set of Practical in Engagement. Per the Balanced in Engagement

---

2. Affinity or "Bridge" groups can gather around board games, sports, food, celebrations, etc.

perspective, pastors may find it advantageous to set as a priority the securing of a mother church to assist in providing funds for a venue.

In the early 1900s, Swedes had diverse responses to the activity of the Holy Spirit and reacted to the spiritual fervor of the newly formed *Pingst* and to the translated writings of Nietzsche in tandem with a growing sense of the inefficacy of the church. Contemporary pluralistic religious expression displays the product of these earlier times in distinguished receptivity of the gospel or disinterest. Sweden's inclination to shift religious allegiance from one faith structure to another in the last millennium is a result of the secularization revealing Christendom as wanting, attempting to quell the voice of the Spirit-empowered church of this past century.

To engage the SSH culture present in Sweden, *Pingst* church planters can find their efforts defaulting to Practical or Spiritual expressions of church multiplication. The perspective of Practical in Engagement, which values venue, social media, and technical production, can reproduce the environment of an excellent church service, tailored to highlight the effort of the implicit Pentecostal undertaking in proclaiming the gospel. Spiritual in Engagement expressions find that public evangelism and sharing about miracles assists in proclaiming the message akin to the examples of Paul in Lystra (Acts 14:8–10). Prayer for miracles to evangelize the unchurched is also a part of this perspective.

A Spirit-empowered, balanced approach to proclaiming the gospel is catalyzed by the baptism in the Holy Spirit, which leads to being sent in mission. Where privacy is accentuated in the affairs of Swedish neighborhoods out of mutual respect, a Pentecostal expression of church multiplication is characterized by the daring to cross over cultural mores to share the gospel. Proclamation, then, is not to be sequestered to buildings but to be carried wherever disciples live, directed implicitly by the Holy Spirit in mission.

Disciples prompted to evangelize their neighbors may find the idea challenging based on how their relationships are currently framed. The Spirit empowers a balanced approach to proclaiming; He leads, sustains and guides the future gathering of the followers of Christ.

Gathering

The third step to the Cycle of Disciple/Church Multiplication is gathering. Jesus gathered those who responded to his proclamation of the message and formed a group that would be set apart for discipleship (Luke 5:11, 5:29, 6:17–19). In the book of Acts, Paul gathered those interested in following

Christ into groups that would become faith communities (Acts 14:27; 16:15, 40). These groups of disciples shared a unified interest in following Christ, which led to shared experiences with Christ as the center of their worship (Acts 2:42–45, 4:4). These gatherings would be the crucibles where disciples could then be developed and sent per the example of Syrian Antioch (Acts 13:1–3) and Athens (Acts 17:16–34).

Disciples who yearned for more of God gathered in the Holiness movement, which provided the foundation for the *Pingst* denomination to form. This impassioned prayer of the Holiness adherents in the early 1900s attracted Lutherans, Baptists, Methodists, Presbyterians, and those of no faith affiliation. In these prayer circles where prayer and fasting also occurred, they sought the baptism in the Holy Spirit and received it. Not only in the early twentieth century but also in the twenty-first century, Spirit-empowered disciples of like minds and hearts gather as the early church once did.

Swedish sociological grouping, as previously mentioned, is crafted through a central point of reference in an activity or figure of interest to an affinity group. While many groups in Sweden may be driven by political motivation and human rights activism, *Pingst* church gatherings may be ill-attended by an SSH. A humanist may be uninterested or cognizant of other Swedish perspectives that draw a spiritual connection to reality.

The field research found that the elevated importance of a venue in Practiced in Engagement (PiE) perspective is to be understood as a part of an attractive church-going experience to the unchurched. This special consideration can be understood as a sort of hospitality. Spiritual in Engagement (SiE) holds that their explicit Pentecostal expressions would invite comments and attract interest (1 Cor 14:22). Both expressions have a propensity to gather disciples, yet exposition of the six most valued Ideal statements regarding church multiplication also empowers the disciple to go to the unchurched without reliance on a church model based on attraction. Participation in sociological groupings outside of church gatherings is important to maintain an incarnate Spirit-empowered, balanced approach to gathering people. Biblical venues of meeting can vary from open-air, public structures to meeting by the river near a city (Acts 16:13–15). The geographic placement of gatherings is not necessarily important in contrast to the orthopathy of the gathering to develop those gathered to grow in Christ. The presence of the Spirit-empowered disciple alongside the unchurched is the goal of the gathering stage, no matter the setting.

Developing

The fourth stage of the Cycle of Disciple/Church Multiplication centers on development. In this stage disciples deepen their devotion to God and further realize his call upon their lives. In conversation, Jesus challenged his disciples to explore his identity, thereby asking Peter, "Who do you say I am?" (Luke 9:20). Prayer to God opens opportunity for the disciple to be influenced in both conversation and conviction by the Holy Spirit (Luke 22:39–42; Acts 1:14). Devotion was present in the life of Jesus as well as in the early church (Luke 4:1–4; Acts 13:1–4). This formative stage, emphasized by time spent in prayer, realigns the disciples of the early church, the 1900s, and the twenty-first century, to receive direction from God. Answers to prayer and fasting can also be found in the bestowment of the baptism in the Holy Spirit for those gathered (Acts 2:1–4). During prayer direction in which path to travel is given (Acts 16:9–10). Prayer times may be spent alone or as part of a group.

Communion with God, the development of the church community, person-to-person, are all of importance (Matt 6:14–15). This interaction provides relational support, which arises from the work of the Holy Spirit in the disciple's life. An extension of this support, networking with other church planters as in the partnership of Timothy and Silas with Paul, can positively affect the health of the faith community. Further, support from a mother church community can assist in encouraging the Cycle of Disciple/Church Multiplication. Communion with God and with other disciples is at the heart of the development of a church. This personal communication helps the disciple and church to maintain a posture of humility while sending missionaries (Acts 16:4–5). In short, the developmental stage prepares disciples and the church for mission.

Both in the early 1900s and in contemporary Sweden, Örebro and Stockholm served as sending bases where disciples were developed and then sent in mission. Motivated by an implicit prompting of the Holy Spirit as a student, the church community provides a place to experience the explicit activity of the Holy Spirit. As school master at *Filadelfiakyrkan* in Stockholm in the late 1930s, Osmin Halldorf endeavored to teach students the rudiments of trusting and living for God in the early twentieth century. Prayer played an integral role in the development of *Pingst* congregations. Older members of *Filadelfiakyrkan* recall prayer meetings in the basements of the church were conducted with such passion that the activity sounded like the buzzing of bees when standing in the sanctuary above. Disciples in the development phase of the Cycle of Disciple/Church Multiplication grow in devotion and spiritual fervency.

A Theory of Pentecostal Church Multiplication among the Unchurched   133

The contemporary field research revealed that the Practical in Engagement perspective grounded half of their top statements in actions of self-effort and in the manipulation of their surroundings. Spiritual in Engagement found that their practices were based on God alone as provider. Scripture helps the disciple to realize that a balance of both God-reliance and self-effort are necessary to participate in *missio Dei*. A Spirit-empowered, balanced approach to the development of the church relies not only on prayer in communication to God, but also on the network of colleagues and authorities within the church.

BIE, PIE, AND SIE AS RELATED TO THE DISCIPLE/CHURCH MULTIPLICATION CYCLE

Each contemporary perspective found that their most valued statements relate to the Cycle of Disciple/Church Multiplication yet with differing emphases. A relationship between the contemporary perspectives and the cycle is necessary to better understand and relate Swedish Church Multiplication to this theory.

Balanced in Engagement in Relation to Disciple/Church Multiplication Cycle

The BiE perspective (see Table 6.1) couches its representative statements in sending (baptizing and sending, mother church, networking, prayer and fasting, baptism in the Holy Spirit), proclaiming (engaging neighbors, prayer and fasting, baptism in the Holy Spirit), gathering (networking, prayer and fasting, baptism in the Holy Spirit), and developing (networking, baptism in the Holy Spirit, prayer and fasting). These statements add to the formation of the disciple to accomplish each stage of the cycle. Baptism in the Holy Spirit can inform each stage, accompanied by actions exemplifying relational direction inward, outward, and upward.

Table 6.1. BiE Statements' Relational Direction and the Disciple/Church Multiplication Cycle

Statement and Direction	Sending	Proclaiming	Gathering	Developing
Mother Church (I)	X			
Networking (I)	X			X
Baptizing and Sending (O)	X			
Engaging Neighbors (O)		X		
Baptism in the Holy Spirit (U)	X	X	X	X
Prayer and Fasting (U)	X	X	X	X

Based on this relational direction, each step of the process requires representation of prayer and fasting and the baptism in the Holy Spirit, coupled with actions of self-effort. Of note is the well-supported stage of sending. Increased attention and resources help to launch a church, and the placement of a mother church in the sending stage provides longevity. Networking with church planters provides opportunity for discipleship. If this relational network is in place, there is a much higher probability that a church will thrive in years to come. The number of statements focused on the sending stage of the cycle implies that deep categorization and effort. While retaining Pentecostal-ness in this perspective, this group confidently identifies as Pentecostal while implementing a tangible, balanced strategy to multiply disciples/churches, informed by interaction with the Holy Spirit. Agreed to the ideal, BiE presents a balanced inward, outward, and upward approach to the cycle. Further investigation into PiE and SiE reveals their perspectives in contrast to the BiE.

Practical in Engagement in Relation to Disciple/Church Multiplication Cycle

In PiE has an even dispersion of relational direction in their statements, yet the representation of statements in the cycle includes both effectively communicating the gospel in an understood manner and sending the church. Replacement of prayer and fasting with praying alone and with others is substantial as it indicates the personal relatability of disciples to each other without the element of fasting.

Inward, outward, and upward relational representation for each perspective is based on the value placed on the sorted statements by each respondent regarding church multiplication. Emphasis on certain statements characterized the values of each perspective, projecting differing practices yet relatively similar emphasis on the activity of the Holy Spirit in church multiplication. PiE presents a balanced inward, outward, and upward relational direction with emphasis on personal connection to the unchurched. In engaging the unchurched, however, PiE perception of the Holy Spirit in the process of church planting is understood by Swedish culture to be more effective as they accentuate a relational and tangible connection to their neighbors.

Table 6.2. PiE Statements' Relational Direction and the Disciple/Church Multiplication Cycle

Statement and Direction	Sending	Proclaiming	Gathering	Developing
Mother Church (I)	X			
Networking (I)	X			X
Read and Explain Scripture (O)		X	X	X
Engaging Neighbors (O)		X		
Baptism in the Holy Spirit (U)	X	X	X	X
Pray alone and with Others (U)	X	X	X	X

Spiritual in Engagement in Relation to Disciple/Church Multiplication Cycle

SiE presents an outward and upward focused perspective, lacking inward organizational strength yet emphasizing spiritual expression (see Table 6.3). SiE lacks representation of statements of inward relational direction, emphasizing outward actions of practice along with upward devotion to God (see Table 6.3). This perspective lacks the integrity of internal fellowship and systems, which may contribute to the necessity of sending. Further, a bolstered emphasis upward toward God is found in their stages of proclaiming, gathering, and developing disciples.

Table 6.3. SiE Statements' Relational Direction and the Disciple/Church Multiplication Cycle

Statement and Direction	Sending	Proclaiming	Gathering	Developing
Baptizing and Sending (O)	X			
Testimonies about God (O)		X		X
Publicly Evangelizing (O)		X		
Praising God for his Grace (U)		X	X	X
Baptism in the Holy Spirit (U)	X	X	X	X
Prayer and Fasting (U)	X	X	X	X

THE THEORY DERIVED

A Spirit-empowered, balanced approach utilizing BiE as a framework would function well as the ideal and practiced method to plant Pentecostal churches to the unchurched of Sweden. Whereas all perspectives found through the Q methods research tool can be considered Spirit-empowered, the agreeance of the respondents on their perspective along with both equal relational direction and implicit/explicit activity of the Holy Spirit confirms BiE as a biblically responsible, culturally relatable model. Interaction with the church and the unchurched while in meaningful relationship with God makes the BiE a culturally acceptable and accessible standard to strive towards while maintaining explicit Pentecostal-ness. This *Pingst* perspective would be effective in reaching the Swedish unchurched through the activity of the Holy Spirit in church multiplication.

THE CYCLE IN PROCESS

Lukan literature showcases encounters between a sent disciple and those who have yet to realize Jesus as Lord. Shared in each instance, the gospel transforms those who choose to trust in Christ. A Spirit-empowered, balanced approach to the cycle increases the efficacy of the efforts of the church planters who are a part of the future of *Pingst*. In the case of the proclamation of Paul to the Ephesians in Acts 19:1–7, Paul (1) is a sent believer who experienced the baptism in the Holy Spirit, being sent as a missionary, (2) proclaims the gospel, relying on God in his inquiry of the Ephesians, and (3) gathers and imparts the baptism of the Holy Spirit to them, leaving them as disciples to further develop and be sent.

The Cycle of Disciple/Church Multiplication provides for the efficiency of the Holy Spirit as equal throughout the choosing of a venue, to the engagement of a neighbor with the gospel, to the baptism and sending of others in mission. The resulting practices of each perspective, however, will need to be understood by the surrounding culture. As a result of the efficiency of the Spirit, implicit pneumatological cues subsequently become explicit in action. Based on the respondent's interviews, the Spirit-empowered, balanced approach to the cycle would produce results more desirable of church planters than the practiced perspectives currently produce. What has been learned through the field research of this study is that what it means to be Pentecostal is defined through both relational direction and implicit/explicit expressions of the activity of the Holy Spirit.

REFLECTIVE INSTRUMENT AND REALIGNMENT

During the field research, respondents repeatedly remarked about the efficacy of the instrument in unearthing their own subjectivity. In conjunction with their observations, respondents hoped that they might utilize the instrument once a year to reflect on what they hold as ideal and then to reveal what is currently practiced. Further, the future inclusion of other staff members in this study was also expressed. The annual implementation of the Ideal and Practice of a *Pingst* pastor engaged in disciple/church multiplication may assist in limiting divergence from the Ideal.

While it is not possible to find out is whether the idealized or practiced perspectives would be more effective based on data derived, a diachronic, longitudinal study through several years can produce findings that may point towards a perspective that yields both disciples sent and fruitful faith communities.

SIGNIFICANCE OF FINDINGS

Data drawn from the contemporary pastors revealed a common vision of what it means to be Pentecostal while planting churches in Sweden. The historical and cultural studies assisted in understanding the diversity among the practices of these pastors in fleshing out the ideal. These findings could contribute to a greater efficacy in the training of pastors to employ the BiE perspective as an ideal and practiced Pentecostal method of planting churches among the unchurched.

Training in Sweden

This study will assist in designing training for church planting in Sweden by accounting and planning for the diversity in practiced perspectives present within *Pingst*. Cultural awareness can shape the way in which a church is planted. Attention to Swedish Secular Humanism (SSH) as a foundational hermeneutic for the culture helps pastors to rely on methods that contextualize Scripture and focus on personal relationships. This expression reveals God as relatable. This can lead to greater numerical adoption of Swedes into faith communities in the initial planting of churches. Presently, this group may display higher efficacy in Pentecostal church planting in popular breadth. The balanced dispersion of inward, outward, and upward statements and personal relational direction emphasized throughout will hopefully appeal to the Swedish Secular Humanist.

In view of biblical and historical examples, church planters must also rely on explicit spiritual expression in establishing churches in Sweden. This emphasis is useful in the spiritual formation of the disciples within a faith community. Conversely, this activity may be a hindrance to the culturally conditioned SSH perspective. This aspect of Pentecostal church planting develops spiritual depth within a faith community.

Awareness of these characteristics can lead to implementation of different leaders at various stages in the lifespan of a disciple or church. PiE pastors may instruct on the initial planting of a church with an emphasis on personal relatability. SiE and mixed pastors may contribute to the integration of spiritual heart once the practical framework of the church plant is constructed. Assessment of the Ideal and Practiced perspectives annually/biennially can support in understanding any shifts in theory and praxis.

Training in Multicultural Europe

Given similar structures in cultural and historical church development, similar understandings of Pentecostal church planting may be found in other European cultures. The secular nature of Europe holds a foundational understanding of pneumatological activity not unlike the SSH.[3] However, each country's church planters may register differing collective emphases in Ideal and Practiced engagement of the unchurched in the Cycle of Disciple/Church Multiplication. A study of contemporary Pentecostal European church planters will assist in constructing a general snapshot of their efforts by revealing their perspectives through the sorting process, respectively.

---

3. Weigel, *Cube and the Cathedral*, 53.

QUESTIONS FOR FURTHER STUDY

1. In which perspective do the denominational leaders within the church planting movement find themselves in the practice of church planting? Is that perspective populated by a majority or minority of current church planting pastors?
2. As a majority of church planters desired that the focus of their church planting team be on the organization of the church, how does this mentality inform the starting of secondary, para-church organizations alongside church planting?
3. Does the presence of secularization in other Western nations (America, Canada) provide opportunity to compare and contrast findings with that of Sweden? Is church planting being affected similarly in these lands?
4. Where this study considered the viewpoint of church planters towards the unchurched, might a research instrument be constructed that endeavors to unearth the pneumatological perspective of the unchurched?
5. Should there be a larger Q set of statements to provide for a granular view of the diversity in perspectives among contemporary Pentecostal church planters?

CONCLUSION

Through a Spirit-empowered, balanced approach to the Cycle of Disciple/Church Multiplication, practices that favored exclusive practicality or spirituality may maintain a more *lagom*,[4] culturally understood way of making disciples. Effective use of the data from the field research instrument can assist the church planter in maintaining a sustainable mobilization of disciples to engage the unchurched of Sweden. Relying on implicit and explicit activity of the Holy Spirit, the Pentecostal respondents found that their desire to reach people must include a balanced strategy to engage the unchurched.

The research showed that church planters know of Christ's instructions, yet the desire to create culturally accessible forms of church can circumvent practicality or spirituality, respectively. Self-adjustment to the ideal will lead to increased efficacy in making disciples, and consequently, planting

---

4. Idiom: moderate or culturally Swedish.

churches. This theory can assist in retaining a closer relationship between ideal and practice when planting Pentecostal faith communities among the unchurched, fulfilling the *missio Dei* with greater precision. A Spirit-empowered, balanced approach to planting Pentecostal churches will appropriately engage the unchurched in the secular context of Sweden.

Appendix A

Demographics of Respondents

Age	Sing./Mar.	Age of Spouse	Kids	Ages of Children	Education	Lead/Staff	Region	Experience	Yrs in Min.	Bap. in HS	Glossolalia	Status of Church
42	m	41	3	9,14,16	examen	lead	urban	planter	20	y	y	closed
	m		2		masters	staff	suburban	planter		y	y	open
42	m	40	2	5,7	gymnasiet	lead	suburban	moth/plant	18	y	y	open
40	m	42	2	5,7	masters	lead	suburban	moth/plant	9	y	y	open
33	m	31	1	4	gymnasiet	staff	medium	planter	10	y	y	closed
31	m	33	1	4	gymnasiet	staff	medium	planter	12	y	y	closed
36	m	35	3	5,7,9	examen	lead	urban	planter	15	y	y	open
35	m		3		masters	lead	urban	planter	5	y	y	closed
48	m	36	1	1	examen	lead	suburban	planter	20	y	y	open
39	m	35	2	7,10	masters	lead	small	planter	20	y	y	open
47	m	43	0		gymnasiet	lead	small	planter	19	y	y	open
46	m	46	4	8,10,14,16	examen	lead	suburban	planter	17	y	y	open
29	m	31	0		gymnasiet	staff	small	moth/plant	9	y	y	open
45	m	43	3	17,18,19	gymnasiet	lead	urban	moth/plant	25	y	y	open
32	m	32	5	2,3,6,7,9	masters	lead	small	planter	17	y	y	open
67	m	69	7	28–44	examen	lead	small	planter	45	y	y	open
50	m	48	3	21,25,26	examen	lead	small	moth/plant	28	y	y	open
45	m	23	3	11,14,15	examen	lead	suburban	planter	20	y	y	open

42	m	40	2	3,7	examen	lead	small	planter	23	y	y	open
36	m	36	1	3,7	gymnasiet	staff	medium	planter	7	y	y	open
50	m	54	3	22,25,27	examen	lead	suburban	moth/plant	30	y	y	open
46	m		2		gymnasiet	lead	small	planter	12	y	y	open
46	m	41	3	10,12,14	examen	staff	urban	planter	25	y	y	open
42	m		3	6,9,11	gymnasiet	lead	small	planter	21	y	y	open
52	m	52	2	27,29	examen	lead	medium	moth/plant	32	y	y	open
52	m	52	2	27,29	examen	lead	medium	moth/plant	32	y	y	open
29	m	30	0		gymnasiet	lead	medium	planter	8	y	y	open
40	m	40	2	6,9	masters	staff	urban	planter	9	y	y	open
40	m	40	3	4,9,11	masters	lead	suburban	moth/plant	20	y	y	open
41	m	43	3	16,14,9	masters	lead	urban	planter	20	y	y	closed

Appendix B

Q Sort Concourse of Statements

1. As a pastor, it is important to pray for others who are in common mission.
2. Christian mission demands that *Pingst* plant churches in unreached areas of Sweden.
3. Gaining inspiration from successful church leaders is an important part of planting a church.
4. A priority in church planting is to find a mother church with which to partner.
5. Reading scripture and explaining its meaning to others is an important part of planting a church.
6. It is important to network with other church planters.
7. Fellowship with other believers is part of church planting.
8. Hearing prophetic words from trusted Christians will in assist planting churches.
9. Technical production of church services is an important part of planting a church.
10. *Pingst* people need to tell others that Jesus Christ is coming back for his church.
11. Sharing testimonies of miracles and healings creates faith.
12. Offering education on the gifts of the Spirit equips the church to proclaim the gospel.

13. Social Media is a key component to church planting.
14. The Baptism in the Holy Spirit is necessary for *Pingst* people to be used in mission.
15. As *Pingst* people we need to send others in mission to neighboring towns.
16. In order to plant churches, we must prepare ourselves to be ready to suffer for the gospel.
17. Establishing a plan for finances for a church plant is very important.
18. As *Pingst* people in church planting mission, we need to remove obstacles which create misunderstanding of Jesus Christ as Savior.
19. As *Pingst* people in God's mission, we need to allow for spontaneous prayer led by God's Holy Spirit.
20. Praising God because of his grace is an important part of the church planting process.
21. *Pingst* needs to communicate more about our collective mission to the world.
22. *Pingst* people must seek opportunities to evangelize people in public.
23. Informing Sweden about false teachers is an important part of mission.
24. To evangelize Sweden, *Pingst* does not need academic education, but needs only the Holy Spirit for guidance.
25. As brothers and sisters in Christ, *Pingst* people need to be recruited to be sent in church planting mission.
26. Praying and fasting is necessary to plant a church.
27. We must baptize people who accept the gospel and send them in mission to the unchurched.
28. As *Pingst* people, we should sell what we have to give to others who might be in need.
29. Spending time with my neighbors where I live is an important part of Christian mission.
30. I am willing to be corrected by the authority over me.
31. So all can hear the gospel, leadership must be organized for equal care to all people.
32. After gathering Christians in Sweden, securing a venue to meet is most important.

33. Involvement of the church with community government and schools is an important part of planting a church.
34. As *Pingst* people, we must seek opportunities to pray for the sick.
35. Volunteering at compassion organizations is an important part of church planting.
36. To plant churches, as *Pingst* people we need to spend time in prayer alone and with others.

Appendix C

Q Sort Concourse Sorted By Intersecting Dimensions

(Key—Se: Self-Reliance; Gr: God-Reliance; Prac: Practical; Cont: Contemporary)

GR-PRAC-BIBLE

- 1. As a Pastor, it is important to pray for others who are in common mission. (Acts 15:33)
- 31. So all can hear the gospel, leadership must be organized for equal care to all people. (Acts 13:43)
- 30. I am willing to be corrected by the authority over me. (Acts 11:18)

GR-PRAC-PINGST

- 2. Christian mission demands that *Pingst* plant churches in unreached areas of Sweden. EH 1919 (*PINGST*)
- 10. *Pingst* people need to tell others that Jesus Christ is coming back for his church. (Rev. 22:7), Boken, Jesus Kommer—Lewi Pethrus (ESCHA.) (*PINGST*)
- 23. Informing Sweden about false teachers is an important part of mission. (2 Peter 2), EH 1919 Antikrist (ESCHA.) (*PINGST*)

GR-PRAC-CONT

- 35. Volunteering at compassion organizations is just as important as church planting.
- 29. Spending time with my neighbors is an important part of Christian mission.
- 33. Involvement of the church with community government and schools is an important part of planting a church.

SE-PRAC-BIBLE

- 11. Sharing testimonies of miracles and healings creates faith. (Acts 9:41) (*PINGST*)
- 22. *Pingst* people must seek opportunities to evangelize people in public. (Acts 3:11–16)
- 28. As *Pingst* people, we should sell what we have to give to others who might be in need. (Acts 2:42–45)

SE-PRAC-PINGST

- 27. We must baptize people who accept the gospel and send them in mission to the unchurched. (Acts 10:48)
- 12. Offering education on the gifts of the Spirit equips the church to proclaim the gospel. EH 1919 (*PINGST*)
- 21. *Pingst* needs to communicate more about our collective mission to the world. EH 1919 (*PINGST*)

SE-PRAC-CONT

- 3. Gaining inspiration from successful church leaders is an important part of planting a church.
- 9. Technical production of church services is an important part of planting a church.

- 13. Social media is a key component to church planting.

GR-IDEAL-BIBLE

- 20. Praising God because of his grace is an important part of the church planting process. (Acts 11:18)
- 8. Hearing prophetic words from trusted Christians will greatly assist planting churches. (Acts 11:28)
- 26. Praying and fasting is necessary to plant a church. (Acts 13:2)

GR-IDEAL-PINGST

- 14. The baptism in the Holy Spirit is necessary for *Pingst* people to be used in mission. (Pethrus at altar, Pethrus on Boat) (*PINGST*)
- 7. Fellowship with other believers is part of church planting. (Acts 2:42–45)
- 24. To evangelize Sweden, *Pingst* does not need academic education, but needs only the Holy Spirit for guidance. (*PINGST*)

GR-IDEAL-CONT

- 6. It is important to network with other church planters. (Acts 15:23–29)
- 19. As *Pingst* people in God's mission, we need to allow for spontaneous prayer led by God's Holy Spirit. (Acts 4:23–31)
- 25. As brothers and sisters in Christ, *Pingst* people need to be recruited to be sent in church planting mission.

SE-IDEAL-BIBLE

- 15. As *Pingst* people we need to send others in mission to neighboring towns. (Acts 11:22)

- 5. Reading Scripture and explaining its meaning to others is an important part of planting a church. (Acts 13:15, 8)
- 18. As *Pingst* people in church planting mission, we need to remove obstacles which create misunderstanding of Jesus Christ as Savior. (Contextualize) (Acts 15:19)

SE-IDEAL-*PINGST*

- 16. In order to plant churches, we must prepare ourselves to be ready to suffer for the gospel. (Pethrus Evangelii Herald Jan 2, 1919) (*PINGST*)
- 34. As *Pingst* people, we must seek opportunities to pray for the sick. (Acts 3:1–10)
- To plant churches, as *Pingst* people we need to spend time in prayer alone and with others. (Pethrus in forest, on boat) (*PINGST*)

SE-IDEAL-CONT

- 4. A priority in church planting is to find a mother church to partner with.
- 17. Establishing a plan for finances for a church plant is very important.
- 32. After gathering Christians in Sweden, securing a venue to meet is most important.

Appendix D

Q Sort Interview Instructions

VERBAL INSTRUCTION: "EACH OF the thirty-six statement cards contains a statement relating to church planting. Please carefully review these statements, then adhere to the following instructions. Please sort these statements in order of importance according to what is most important in the ideal way to plant a *Pingst* church in Sweden which reaches the unchurched."

1. First sort them into three piles: One pile of great importance, one pile of indifference, one pile of least importance.
2. Second, begin to place them on the grid, starting with three cards representing what you believe to be the most important statements to observe (place card on the far right of the grid under "+4," working vertically downward to fill the column) and then choose three cards from representing what is least important and place them on the far left of the grid under "-4."
3. Sort the cards onto the rest of the target grid in order of most importance to least importance.
4. Procedural steps after the first sort: Record the sort. Ask why the 3 most and 3 least important statements are in their locations. Collect the statements. Ask the subject to do a second and final sort of the statements based on the following question.

Second Sort: Please sort these statements again. Sort them in order of what you actually practiced according to your time and values in planting a *Pingst* church in Sweden which reaches the unchurched.

The same sorting instructions will be followed, yet the second sort will be conducted based on what was practiced most and least in church planting.

Procedural steps after the second sort: Record the sort. Ask why the three most and three least important statements are in their locations.

Follow-Up Question: Did you learn something from this sorting/interview experience?

Appendix E

Q Sort Target Grid and Interview

Name:
Age:
Relationship: Single Married
If Married: Age of Spouse
Kids: Number Ages
Edu: Examen Masters Doktorand
Pastor: Lead Staff
Region: Rural Small Town Suburban Urban
Experience: Planter/Planning/Mother Church/Not Planning
Years in Ministry:
Baptized in the Holy Spirit: Yes No
Speak in Tongues: Yes No

Ideal Sort Results:

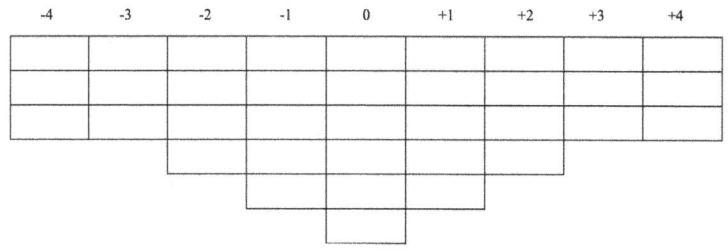

Why the three Most Agreed were chosen?
Why the three Most Disagreed were chosen?

Practiced Sort Results:

-4	-3	-2	-1	0	+1	+2	+3	+4

Why the three Most Agreed were chosen? Why the three Most Disagreed were chosen?

Did you learn something? What?

Appendix F

Q Sort Ideal Single-Factor Analysis

Factor Matrix with an X Indicating a Defining Sort

Loadings—QSORT
1 -i 0.3439
2 -i 0.6993X
3 -i 0.8132X
4 -i 0.6567X
5 -i 0.6514
6 -i 0.6959X
7 -i 0.7576X
8 -i 0.7811X
9 -i 0.6890X
10 -i 0.7599X
11 -i 0.7904X
12 -i 0.6659X
13 -i 0.7429X
14 -i 0.5756
15 -i 0.8181X
16 -i 0.4678
17 -i 0.7859X
18 -i 0.6961X
19 -i 0.5587X
20 -i 0.6751X
21 -i 0.5467X

22 -i 0.4348
23 -i 0.6215X
24 -i 0.6644X
25 -i 0.5877X
26 -i 0.7085X
27 -i 0.7012X
28 -i 0.3901
29 -i 0.6380X
30 -i 0.5365X

% expl. Var . . . 44

Appendix G

Q Sort Practiced Two-Factor Analysis

FACTOR MATRIX WITH AN X INDICATING A DEFINING SORT

Loadings—QSORT
1 -p 0.0647 -0.5274X
2 -p 0.2881 -0.1401
3 -p 0.6166 -0.4001
4 -p 0.4949 -0.3031
5 -p 0.7209X -0.3950
6 -p 0.7086X -0.2752
7 -p 0.6694X 0.2099
8 -p 0.5069X 0.0682
9 -p 0.5684X -0.1240
10 -p 0.6633X -0.1178
11 -p 0.4969X -0.0871
12 -p 0.5440X 0.1634
13 -p 0.4966X -0.2376
14 -p 0.0646 0.7450X
15 -p 0.4644X 0.1442
16 -p 0.5070X 0.2218
17 -p 0.7157X -0.3076
18 -p 0.3507 0.7316X
19 -p 0.3939 0.6521X

20 -p 0.5858X 0.0092
21 -p 0.3675 -0.4717
22 -p 0.5302X 0.2343
23 -p 0.7092X -0.1673
24 -p 0.4151 0.5825
25 -p 0.6414X 0.0504
26 -p 0.7240X 0.0905
27 -p 0.6188X -0.2141
28 -p 0.4812X -0.2429
29 -p 0.2941 0.3047
30 -p 0.5285X -0.1968

% expl. Var . . . 29 12

Appendix H

Q Sort Second-Order Analysis of Ideal, Practice 1, Practice

CORRELATION MATRIX BETWEEN SORTS

SORTS 1 2 3

1 *Pingst_i* 100 83 53
2 *PingstP*1 83 100 19
3 *Pingst_s* 53 19 100

Unrotated Factor Matrix
Factors
1 2 3
SORTS
1 *Pingst_i* 0.9254 0.0018 0.3791
2 *PingstP*1 0.5628 -0.0040 0.0000
3 *Pingst_s* 0.3551 0.6033 0.0000

Eigenvalues 1.2991 0.3640 0.1437
% expl.Var. . . . 43 12 5

Cumulative Communalities Matrix
Factors 1 Thru . . .

          1 2 3
SORTS
1 *Pingst_*i 0.8563 0.8563 1.0000
2 *Pingst*P1 0.3167 0.3167 0.3167
3 *Pingst_*s 0.1261 0.4900 0.4900

cum% expl.Var. . . 43 55 60
Factor Matrix with an X Indicating a Defining Sort
Loadings—QSORT 1 2

1 *Pingst_*i 0.9254X 0.0018
2 *Pingst*P1 0.5628X -0.0040
3 *Pingst_*s 0.3551 0.6033X
% expl.Var. . . 43 12

Appendix I

Consent Sent to Research Respondents

THANK YOU FOR YOUR voluntary participation in the research study at *Pingst* Pastor this past January 2018! I am very pleased with the gathering of data which will assist our church planting efforts in *Pingst* as we partner together to reach Sweden. I am in the data-analysis phase, so there are no conclusions yet, but I am grateful for the fascinating data.

I failed to give you a few assurances in writing at the time of your participation, so I'm doing it now. This doesn't require you to do anything unless you have a concern about the study. In case you do have concerns, see below for contact options.

First, I want to assure you that the personal information you provided will be kept anonymous. Confidentiality and security are important to me as a researcher and to the institution I am working through for the doctoral program. *Pingst* shares this concern, and I'd like for you to feel confident in this research as a participant.

Second, I wanted you to know that in addition to my doctoral committee and the Institutional Review Board at Evangel University, this research was approved by Daniel Alm, Ulrik Josefsson, and Nicklas Mörling.

You have the right to withdraw from this research at any time. If you have any concerns regarding the handling of your data, feel free to email myself or the coordinator for my program at the email below.

Together we serve the Lord, Thank you again.
Phil Zarns

IRB contact: For research-related problems or questions regarding ethical research practices, the AGTS-IDS-IRB may be contacted through the Intercultural Doctoral Studies Program Coordinator, Evangel University, 1435 N Glenstone, Springfield, MO 65802 (email: AGTS-IDS-IRB@evangel.edu).

Bibliography

Ahlstrand, Love. "Många Flyktingar Söker Sig Till Sverige—Trots Nya Åtgärder." *Dagens Nyheter*, November 27, 2015. http://www.dn.se/nyheter/sverige/manga-flyktingar-soker-sig-till-sverige-trots-nya-atgarder-1/.
Alcala, Jesús. "Humanisterna Tiger Om Grunden För Sin Tro." *Svenska Dagbladet*, May 22, 2010. https://www.svd.se/humanisterna-tiger-om-grunden-for-sin-tro.
Allen, Roland. *Missionary Methods: St. Paul's or Ours?: A Study of the Church in the Four Provinces*. Cambridge, UK: Lutterworth, 2012.
———. *The Spontaneous Expansion of the Church and the Causes Which Hinder It*. 1st American ed. Grand Rapids: Eerdmans, 1962.
Alm, Daniel. Interview on church planting by Phil Zarns, 2015.
Alvarsson, Jan-Åke, Annica Björk, Olof Djurfeldt, Björne Erixon, Ivar Lundgren, Gunilla Nyberg Oskarsson, Nils-Eije Stävare, and Magnus Wahlström. *Pingströrelsen*. Edited by Claes Waern. 2 vols. Vol. 1, Örebro, Sweden: Libris, 2007.
Anderson, Amy S. *When You Come Together*. Raleigh, NC: Being Church, 2011.
Andersen, Erik. "Början, Glöd Från Altaret." *Glöd från Altaret*, February 11, 1909.
Anderson, Christina, and John F. Burns. "Stockholm Hit by Blasts after Threatening Message." *New York Times*, December 11, 2010. https://www.nytimes.com/2010/12/12/world/europe/12sweden.html.
Anderson, Ray. S. *Ministry on the Fireline: A Practical Theology for an Empowered Church*. Eugene, OR: Wipf & Stock, 2011.
Salvation Army. "The Salvation Army International—Sweden and Latvia." https://www.salvationarmy.org/ihq/swedenlatvia.
Aronson, Torbjorn. "Spirit and Church in the Ecclesiology of Lewi Pethrus." *Theology* 11/2 (2012) 18.
Arrington, French L., and Roger Stronstad. *Full Life Bible Commentary to the New Testament: An International Commentary for Spirit-Filled Christians*. Grand Rapids: Zondervan, 1999.
Arthur, Eddie. "Missiology: Missio Dei and the Mission of the Church." Wycliffe Global Alliance. http://www.wycliffe.net/missiology?id=3960#_ftn3.
Asker, Anna. "Gud ett Måste vid Kyrkobröllop." *Svenska Dagbladet*, May 30, 2004.
Bak, Krzysztof. "Svenska Studenter har alla Svar—men inga Frågor—Dn.se." March 11, 2013.
Barratt, Thomas Ball. "Början, Glöd Från Altaret." *Glöd från Altaret*, January 1, 1910.
Bauckham, Richard. *Bible and Mission: Christian Witness in a Postmodern World*. Grand Rapids: Baker Academic, 2003.

Bibliography

Beaver, R. Pierce. *Perspectives on the World Christian Movement: A Reader.* Edited by Ralph D. Winter and Steven C. Hawthorne. Pasadena, CA: William Carey Library, 1981.

Beggs, Greg. *Indigenous Principles and Partnership.* Mission, Vision, and Core Values: Rpts Missiology Series 1. Springfield, MO: Assemblies of God World Missions, 2016.

Berger, Peter. *The Sacred Canopy: Elements of a Sociological Theory of Religion.* New York: Open Road, 2011.

———. *The Social Construction of Reality.* London: Penguin, 1966.

Berggren, Henrik, and Lars Trägårdh. *Är Svensken Människa?: Den Svenska Individualismens Historia* [Is a Swede Human?: The Swedish History of Individualism]. Stockholm: Norstedts, 2014.

Bergstedt, Anders. "Terrorattacken blev Vändpunkt för Polisen—Dn.Åsikt.» *Dagens Nyheter*, April 11, 2017. http://asikt.dn.se/asikt/debatt/terrorattacken-blev-vandpunkt-for-polisen/.

Bevans, Stephen B. *Models of Contextual Theology.* Maryknoll, NY: Orbis, 2002.

Bosch, David J. *Transforming Mission: Paradigm Shifts in Theology of Mission.* Maryknoll, NY: Orbis, 1991.

Bose, Raj C. "A Note on Fisher's Inequality for Balanced Incomplete Block Designs." In English. *Ann. Math. Statist.* 20/4 (1949) 619–20.

Bromgard, Gregg, Christopher Linn, and David Trafimow. "Janteloven and the Expression of Pride in Norway and the United States." *Journal of Social Psychology* 154 (2014) 375–78.

Bruce, Frederick F. *The Book of Acts.* Grand Rapids: Eerdmans, 1988.

Bundy, David. *Visions of Apostolic Mission: Scandinavian Pentecostal Mission to 1935.* Uppsala, Sweden: Uppsala Universitet, 2009.

———. "Social Ethics in the Church of the Poor: The Cases of T. B. Barratt and Lewi Pethrus." Essay presented for the EPCRA conference, Leuven, Belgium, 2001.

By, Ulrika. "Ensamvarg eller inte? Inget går ännu att Utesluta—Dn.Se." *Dagens Nyheter*, April 11, 2017. http://www.dn.se/sthlm/ensamvarg-eller-inte-inget-gar-annu-att-utesluta/.

Byström, Malin. "Han Botades från Diabetes." *Aftonbladet*, June 19, 2002.

Carlsson, Carl-Gustav. *Människan, Samhället, Och Gud. Grunddrag I Lewi Pethruskristendomsuppfattning* [People, Community and God]. Insamlingsstiftelsen FöR Pingstforskning 15. Stockholm: Pingst, 2012.

Carson, Donald A. *Christ and Culture Revisited.* Grand Rapids: Eerdmans, 2008.

Childress, Gavin. *Opening Up Luke's Gospel.* Carlisle, PA: Day One, 2006.

Clark, Maudemarie, and Robert B. Pippin. *Nietzsche on Truth and Philosophy.* Cambridge, UK: Cambridge University Press, 1990.

Coleman, Robert, and Billy Graham. *The Master Plan of Evangelism.* 2nd ed., abridged. Grand Rapids: Baker, 2010.

Costas, Orlando E. *Christ Outside the Gate: Mission Beyond Christendom.* Maryknoll, NY: Orbis, 1982.

Council for Secular Humanism. "A Secular Humanist Declaration—Council for Secular Humanism." News release, 1980. https://www.secularhumanism.org/index.php/11.

General Council of the Assemblies of God. "History of the Assemblies of God." http://ag.org/top/About/History/index.cfm.

Bibliography 165

Cowdell, Scott. *Is Jesus Unique?: A Study of Recent Christology.* Mahwah, NJ: Paulist, 1996.

Dahlbäck, Göran, and Lars Nilsson. *Staden På Vattnet: 1252–1850* [City on the Water: 1252–1850]. Stockholm: Stockholmia, 2002.

Davidsson, Tommy. *Lewi Pethrus' Ecclesiological Thought 1911–1974: A Transdenominational Pentecostal Ecclesiology.* Boston: Brill, 2015.

Dowsett, Rose. *Global Mission: Reflections and Case Studies in Contextualization for the Whole Church.* Pasadena, CA: William Carey Library, 2011.

Easton, Matthew G. *Easton's Bible Dictionary.* New York: Harper, 1893.

Elmer, Duane. *Cross-Cultural Connections: Stepping Out and Fitting In around the World.* Downers Grove, IL: InterVarsity, 2009.

———. *Cross-Cultural Servanthood: Serving the World in Christlike Humility.* Downers Grove, IL: InterVarsity, 2009.

Engeli, Isabel, and Christoffer Green-Pedersen, and L. T. Larsen. *Morality Politics in Western Europe: Parties, Agendas and Policy Choices.* Basingstoke, UK: Palgrave Macmillan, 2012.

Engelsviken, Tormod. "Missio Dei: The Understanding and Misunderstanding of a Theological Concept in European Churches and Missiology." *International Review of Mission* 92/4 (2003) 481–97.

Enquist, Per Olov. *Lewi's Journey.* 1st ed. New York: Overlook Duckworth, 2005.

Erikson, Erik H., and Joan M. Erikson. *The Life Cycle Completed.* Extended version. New York: Norton, 1998.

Eusebius. *Ecclesiastical History.* Translated by Paul L. Maier. New York: Stanford & Swords, 1850.

Fee, Gordon D. *Paul, the Spirit, and the People of God.* Grand Rapids: Baker, 1994.

Fernando, Ajith. *Acts.* NIV Application Commentary. Grand Rapids: Zondervan, 2010.

Fielding, Nigel G., and Jane L. Fielding. *Linking Data.* Minneapolis: Sage, 1986.

Fitzmyer, Joseph A. *The Acts of the Apostles.* Anchor Bible 31. New York: Doubleday, 1998.

Flynn, Tom. "Secular Humanism Defined—Council for Secular Humanism." Council for Secular Humanism, https://www.secularhumanism.org/index.php/13.

Forrest, James E. "Guds Församling." *Evangelii Trumpet* 4/6 (June 1, 1905).

Fowler, James W. *Stages of Faith: The Psychology of Human Development.* New York: HarperCollins, 1995.

Gallagher, Robert L. *Mission in Acts: Course Manual.* Wheaton, IL: Wheaton College, 2017.

———. *Missionary Methods: Research, Reflections, and Realities.* Edited by Craig Ott and J. D. Payne. Pasadena, CA: William Carey Library, 2013.

Gallagher, Robert L., and Paul Hertig. *Mission in Acts: Ancient Narratives in Contemporary Context.* American Society of Missiology Series. Maryknoll, NY: Orbis, 2004.

Gäreskog, Marianne, and Roland Gäreskog. *Lewi Pethrus I Konflikt: Om Några Konflikter år 1929 Mellan Lewi Pethrus och Kända Personer inom Pingströrelsen.* Alvik: Pingst, 2006.

Gibbs, Eddie. *In Name Only.* Pasadena, CA: Fuller Seminary, 2000.

Horton, Stanley M. *Acts.* The Complete Biblical Library 6. Springfield, MO: Gospel Publishing House, 1991.

Gilliland, Dean. *The Word Among Us: Contextualizing Theology for Mission Today.* Eugene, OR: Wipf & Stock, 2002.

Glasner, Peter E. *The Sociology of Secularisation: A Critique of a Concept.* Abingdon, UK: Routledge and Kegan Paul, 1977.

Grenz, Stanley J. *A Primer on Postmodernism.* Grand Rapids,: Eerdmans, 1996.

Grunlan, Stephen A., and Marvin K. Mayers. *Cultural Anthropology: A Christian Perspective.* Grand Rapids: Academie, 1988.

Gustaffsson, Alfred. "Brudgummans Röst Annonsering." *Evangelii Härold*, 1917.

Gustafsson, Algot. "Början, Glöd Från Altaret." *Glöd från Altaret*, 1909.

Hall, Edward T. *The Dance of Life: The Other Dimension of Time.* New York: Peter Smith, 1996.

Halldorf, Joel. "'En Församling i Varje Stad.' Ideal för Lokal Församlingsverksamhet I 1900-Talets Svenska Pingströrelse." In *Församlingsplantering i Pingst*, edited by Ulrik Josefsson and Magnus Wahlström. Alvik, Sweden: Institutet för Pentekostala Studier, 2015.

———. *Pentecostal Politics in a Secular World" The Life and Leadership of Lewi Pethrus.* Cham, Switzerland: Palgrave Macmillan, 2020.

Halldorf, Joel, Göran Lennartsson, Ulrik Josefsson, Carolina Nilsson, Andreas K. G. Thörn, Magnus Wahlström, and Fredrik Wenell. *Församlingsplantering I Pingst: Rapport Från ett Forskningsprojekt på IPS 2015.* Edited by Ulrik Josefsson and Magnus Wahlström. Alvik: Institutet för Pentekostala Studier, 2016.

Halldorf, Joel, Fredrik Wenell, and Stanley Hauerwas. *Between the State and the Eucharist: Free Church Theology in Conversation with William T. Cavanaugh.* Eugene, OR: Wipf & Stock, 2014.

Hartwick, A. Reuben. "Enrichment Journal." General Council of the Assemblies of God, http://enrichmentjournal.ag.org/top/holyspirit_articledisplay.cfm?targetBay=1b574def-b227-4617-bfc7-a02cdb926902&ModID=2&Process=DisplayArticle&RSS_RSSContentID=15175&RSS_OriginatingChannelID=1170&RSS_Originating RSSFeedID=4486&RSS_Source=.

Hesselgrave, David F., Donald A. McGavran, and Jeff Reed. *Planting Churches Cross-Culturally: North America and Beyond.* Grand Rapids: Baker, 2000.

Hesselgrave, David J., and Edward Rommen. *Contextualization: Meanings, Methods, and Models.* Pasadena, CA: William Carey Library, 2000.

Hiebert, Paul G. "Conversion, Culture and Cognitive Categories." *Gospel in Context*, October 1, 1978.

———. "Critical Contextualization." *International Bulletin of Mission Research* 11/3 (July 1987) 8.

———. "The Flaw of the Excluded Middle." *Missiology: An International Review* 10/1 (1982) 12.

———. *Transforming Worldviews: An Anthropological Understanding of How People Change.* Grand Rapids: Baker, 2008.

Hoedemaker, Libertus A. "The Legacy of J. C. Hoekendijk." *International Bulletin of Mission Research* 19/4 (1995) 166–70.

Hoekendijk, Johannes C. *The Missionary Structures of the Congregation.* Uppsala, Sweden: The World Council of Churches, 1968.

Hofstede, Geert. "Sweden." ITIM International, https://geert-hofstede.com/sweden.html.

Hofstede, Geert, Gert Jan Hofstede, and M. Minkov. *Cultures and Organizations: Software of the Mind*. 3rd ed. Columbus, OH: McGraw-Hill Education, 2010.

Holmberg, Mats. "Lär Dig Konsten Att Rätt Fira Pingst. Gift Dig. Tala I Tungor. Men Med Förnuft—Dn.Se." *Dagens Nyheter*, May 21, 1994.

Humanisterna. "Humanisternas Idéprogram." http://www.humanisterna.se/human isternas-ideprogram/.

Hunter, George G. *The Celtic Way of Evangelism: How Christianity Can Reach the West—Again*. Nashville, TN: Abingdon, 2010.

Hunter, James D. *To Change the World: The Irony, Tragedy and Possibility of Christianity in the Late Modern World*. Oxford, UK: Oxford University Press, 2010.

Janson, Larseric. "Lewi Pethrus på Vargön.» In *Arkivmaterial* 52:06. Stockholm, 1972.

Johansson, Fredrik. "Sd-Nej Till Flyktingar." *Värnamo Nyheter*, October 4, 2015.

John Paul II, Pope. "Address of John Paul II to the Plenary Council 'Cor Unum.'" In *The Holy See*, edited by the Holy Catholic Church. Vatican City: Libreria Editrice Vaticana, 2002.

Johnson, Alan R. *Apostolic Function in 21st Century Missions*. Pasadena, CA: William Carey Library, 2009.

Johnstone, Patrick. *The Future of the Global Church: History, Trends and Possibilities*. Milton Keynes, UK: Authentic, 2011.

Jones, Lauren Said-Moorhouse and Bryony. "Dazed but Defiant, Stockholm Unites after Attack." *CNN*, April 8, 2017. http://www.cnn.com/2017/04/08/europe/sweden-truck-attack-aftermath/index.html.

Jonker, Louis.C. *Global Hermeneutics?: Reflections and Consequences*. Edited by Knut Holter and Louis.C. Jonker. International Organization for the Study of the Old Testament. Atlanta: Society of Biblical Literature, 2010.

Josefsson, Ulrik. "Liv Och Över Nog." Dissertation, Lund University, 2005.

Kärkkäinen, Veli-Matti. *The Holy Spirit: A Guide to Christian Theology*. Louisville, KY: Westminster John Knox, 2012.

———. *Pneumatology: The Holy Spirit in Ecumenical, International, and Contextual Perspective*. Grand Rapids: Baker, 2002.

Keener, Craig. S. *Acts: An Exegetical Commentary*. 4 vols. Grand Rapids: Baker, 2012–2015.

———. *3 Crucial Questions About the Holy Spirit*. 3 Crucial Questions. Grand Rapids: Baker, 1996.

Kent, Neil. *The Soul of the North: A Social, Architectural and Cultural History of the Nordic Countries, 1700–1940*. London: Reaktion, 2001.

Kistemaker, Simon J. *Exposition of the Acts of the Apostles*. Grand Rapids: Baker, 1990.

Koeshall, Anita. *Redeemed Power and Dynamic Asymmetry*. Saarbrücken, Germany: LAP Lambert Academic, 2012.

Koeshall, Anita, and John Koeshall. "Ecclesiology-to-Go: Discerning Church in SFC (and Other Unexpected Forms and Places)." In *J. Philip Hogan Series*. Springfield, MO: Assemblies of God Theological Seminary, 2010.

Kraft, Charles H., and Dean S. Gilliland. *Appropriate Christianity*. Pasadena, CA: William Carey Library, 2005.

Kraft, Charles H., and Marguerite G. Kraft. *Christianity in Culture: A Study in Dynamic Biblical Theologizing in Cross Cultural Perspective*. Maryknoll, NY: Orbis, 2005.

Kraus, Steven E. "Research Paradigms and Meaning Making: A Primer." *The Qualitative Report* 10/4 (2005) 758–70.

Landes, David. "Swedish Church Members 'Don't Believe in Jesus." *The Local*, June 15, 2011. http://www.thelocal.se/20110615/34370.

LaPoorta, Japie. *The Globalization of Pentecostalism: A Religion Made to Travel*. Edited by Murray Dempster, Byron D. Klaus, and Douglas Petersen. Eugene, OR: Wipf & Stock, 2011.

Lewis, Paul. *Missiological Research: Interdisciplinary Foundations, Methods, and Integration*. Edited by Martin Gilbert, Alan Johnson, and Paul Lewis. Pasadena, CA: William Carey, 2018.

Lingenfelter, Sherwood G. *Transforming Culture: A Challenge for Christian Mission*. Grand Rapids: Baker, 1998.

Loder, James E. *The Logic of the Spirit: Human Development in Theological Perspective*. 1st ed. San Francisco: Jossey-Bass, 1998.

———. *The Transforming Moment*. 2nd ed. Colorado Springs, CO: Helmers & Howard, 1989.

Luzbetak, Louis J. *The Church and Cultures: New Perspectives in Missiological Anthropology*. Maryknoll, NY: Orbis, 1989.

Löfgren, Emma. "Why Most Swedes Don't Care About National Day." *The Local*, June 5, 2015. https://www.thelocal.se/20150605/why-dont-swedes-care-for-the-national-day.

Malina, Bruce J. *The New Testament World: Insights from Cultural Anthropology*. Louisville: Westminster John Knox, 2001.

Maynet, Roland. *Rhetorical Argumentation in Biblical Texts: Essays from the Lund 2000 Conference*. Edited by Anders Eriksson, Thomas H. Olbricht and Walter Übelacker. London: Bloomsbury, 2002.

McClung, L. Grant, Jr. *The Globalization of Pentecostalism: A Religion Made to Travel*. Edited by M. Dempster, B. D. Klaus, and D. Petersen. Eugene, OR: Wipf & Stock, 2011.

McCracken, Grant David. *The Long Interview*. Qualitative Research Methods. Newbury Park, CA: Sage, 1988.

Menzies, Robert. *Empowered for Witness*. Academic paperback. New York: Bloomsbury, 2004.

Migrationsverket. "Migration—Statistics." http://www.migrationsverket.se/English/About-the-Migration-Agency/Facts-and-statistics-/Statistics.html.

Miller, Denzil R. *Empowered for Global Mission: A Mission-Pneumatological Investigation of Acts*. Springfield, MO: Assemblies of God Theological Seminary, 2005.

Miller, Stephen M. *Who's Who and Where's Where*. Uhrichsville, OH: Barbour, 2012.

Mitchell, Richard G. *Secrecy and Fieldwork*. Minneapolis: Sage, 1993.

Mittelstadt, Martin W. *Reading Luke-Acts in the Pentecostal Tradition: Reflections on the History and Status of Research*. Cleveland: CPT, 2010.

Moberg, Jessica. *Charismatic Christianity in Finland, Norway, and Sweden: Case Studies in Historical and Contemporary Developments*. Edited by Jessica Moberg and Jane Skjoldli. New York: Springer, 2018.

Moltmann, Jürgen. *The Church in the Power of the Spirit: A Contribution to Messianic Ecclesiology*. Minneapolis: Fortress, 1977.

Moore, Russell. *The Kingdom of Christ: The New Evangelical Perspective*. Wheaton, IL: Crossway, 2004.

Mörling, Niklas. Interview on church planting by Phil Zarns, January 4, 2018.

Netland, Harold. *Encountering Religious Pluralism: The Challenge to Christian Faith & Mission.* Downers Grove, IL: InterVarsity, 2001.
Neuman, Scott. "He, She or Hen? Sweden's New Gender-Neutral Pronoun." *The Two Way*, NPR, March 27, 2015. http://www.npr.org/sections/thetwo-way/2015/03/27/395785965/he-she-or-hen-sweden-s-new-gender-neutral-pronoun.
Newbigin, Leslie. *The Gospel in a Pluralist Society.* Grand Rapids: Eerdmans, 1989.
Nida, Eugene A. *Customs and Cultures: Anthropology for Christian Missions.* Pasadena, CA: William Carey Library, 1975.
Niebuhr, H. Richard. *Christ and Culture.* Manhattan: Harper, 1956.
———. *The Social Sources of Denominationalism.* New York: World, 1957.
Norén, Stellan. "Lewi Pethrus Ättlingar Samlas I Nora I Dag." *Nerikes Allehanda*, August 21, 2015. http://www.na.se/slakt-o-vanner/lewi-pethrus-attlingar-samlas-i-nora-i-dag.
Nunes, John. *Wittenberg Meets the World.* Grand Rapids: Eerdmans, 2017.
O'Brien, Zoie, Patrick Christys, Lizzie Stromme, and Will Kirby. "Sweden Terror: Suspect Arrested Following Manhunt in Stockholm." *Express*, April 8, 2017. https://www.express.co.uk/news/world/789219/Sweden-terror-truck-attack-Drottninggatan-Parliament-closed.
Ögren, Anders. *The Swedish Financial Revolution.* London: Palgrave Macmillan, 2016.
Ong, Walter J., and John Hartley. *Orality and Literacy: The Technologizing of the Word.* New York: Routledge, 2012.
Ostwalt, Conrad. *Secular Steeples: Popular Culture and the Religious Imagination.* 2nd ed. New York: Bloomsbury, 2012.
Ottestig, Johannes. "Helad Av Gud—Men Sen Då?" *Dagen*, June 7, 2013.
———. "Liberala Debattören Fredrik Segerfeldt Vill Inte Att Kristna Ska Kalla Sig Kristna—Dagen.Se." *Dagen*, March 15, 2017. http://www.dagen.se/liberala-debattoren-fredrik-segerfeldt-vill-inte-att-kristna-ska-kalla-sig-kristna-1.938238.
Park, Nick. *Ministry to Migrants and Asylum Seekers.* Kindle ed. Dublin: Evangelical Alliance Ireland, 2015.
Peterson, David G. *The Acts of the Apostles.* Grand Rapids: Eerdmans, 2009.
Peterson, Therese. "Lewi Pethrus—Vem Var Han?" *Dagen*, September 4, 2009. http://www.dagen.se/livsstil/lewi-pethrus-vem-var-han-1.182801.
Pethrus, Lewi. "Brudgummans Röst." *Brudgummans Röst*, 1911.
———. *Christian Church Discipline.* Chicago: Filadelfia, 1944.
———. "Den Nytestamentliga Enhetstanken." *Evangelii Härold*, 1941.
———. "En Kontingent Flyktingar Från Finland." *Evangelii Härold*, 1940.
———. "Filadelfiaförsamlingens I Stockholm Räddningsmission." *Evangelii Härold*, January 5, 1916, 1.
———. "Gåfvor Till Oscarsbergs BarnHem in Rönnlnge." *Evangelii Härold*, January 5, 1916, 1.
———. "Jesus Kommer." *Evangelii Härold* 1/1 (1915) 4.
———. *Lewi Pethrus: A Spiritual Memoir.* Plainfield, NJ: Logos, 1973.
———. "Löftena Kunna Ej Svika." 1913.
———. *The Wind Bloweth Where It Listeth.* Minneapolis: Bethany Fellowship, 1945.
Piensoho, Niklas. *100 Dagar Med Jesus.* Örebro, Sweden: Libris, 2013.
Pierson, Paul E. *The Dynamics of Christian Mission: History through a Missiological Perspective.* Pasadena, CA: William Carey International University Press, 2009.

Pingst. "Församlingsplantering—Pingst." https://www.pingst.se/sverige/forsamlingsplantering/.

———. "Om Pingst—About Pingst." https://www.pingst.se/om-pingst/.

Porter, Stanley E. *Paul: Jew, Greek, and Roman*. Pauline Studies 5. Leiden, Netherlands: Brill, 2008.

Puranen, Bi. "WV6 Results Sweden 2011." Stockholm: Institute for Future Studies, 2016.

Ratzka, Adolf. "Eradication of 'Deviants': The Dark Side of the Swedish Model." Stockholm: Independent Living Institute, 1997. https://www.independentliving.org/docs5/sterilization.html.

Regeringskansliet, Regeringen och. "Statement by Prime Minister Stefan Löfven in Connection with the Incident in Stockholm." April 11, 2017. http://www.government.se/statements/2017/04/statement-by-prime-minister-stefan-lofven-in-connection-with-the-incident-in-stockholm/.

Report, Willowbrook. *Perspectives on the World Christian Movement: A Reader*. Edited by Ralph D. Winter and Steven C. Hawthorne. Pasadena, CA: William Carey Library, 1981.

Ringkvist, Rickard. "Åsa Waldau: Det Går Inte Att Förlåta Pingströrelsen." *Dagen*, October 13, 2009.

Robert, Dana.L. *Occupy until I Come: A. T. Pierson and the Evangelization of the World*. Grand Rapids: Eerdmans, 2003.

Rodgers, Darrin. *Northern Harvest: Pentecostalism in North Dakota*. Bismarck, ND: North Dakota District of the Assemblies of God, 2003.

———. "Prominent Novelist Sven Lidman Shocked Sweden by 1921 Conversion to Pentecostalism." Flower Pentecostal Heritage Center, March 16, 2015. https://ifphc.wordpress.com/2015/03/16/prominent-novelist-sven-lidman-shocked-sweden-by-1921-conversion-to-pentecostalism/.

Rogers, Everett M., and Thomas M. Steinfatt. *Intercultural Communication*. Prospect Heights, IL: Waveland, 1999.

Rojas, Mauricio. *Beyond the Welfare State*. Stockholm, Sweden: Timbro, 2001.

———. *Sweden after the Swedish Model: From Tutorial State to Enabling State*. Translated by Roger Tanner and Cristina Edbrooke. Stockholm: Timbro, 2005.

Rousseau, Jean-Jacques. *The Social Contract & Discourses*. Ann Arbor, MI: Joseph M. Dent, 1920.

RPTM. "Stadgar—Ideella Föreningar." Skatteverket, https://www.skatteverket.se/foretagochorganisationer/foreningar/ideellaforeningar/starta/stadgar.4.70ac421612e2a997f85800028440.html.

Rynkiewich, Michael. *Soul, Self, and Society: A Postmodern Anthropology for Mission in a Postcolonial World*. Eugene, OR: Cascade, 2012.

Sage. "Editor Guidelines:Ethics Approval and Informed Consent Statements." 2018. https://uk.sagepub.com/sites/default/files/editor_guidelines.pdf.

Sandberg, Anna Bieniaszewski. "Del 1: "För Att Bygga Guds Verk Krävs En Stark Ekonomi."" *Dagen*, January 2, 2008.

Sanders, Ed P. *Judaism: Practice and Belief, 63 BCE–66 CE*. London: SCM, 1992.

Schulman, Salomon. "Tungor Såsom Av Eld." *Dagens Nyheter*, June 3, 2006.

Shaw, R. Daniel, and Charles E. van Engen. *Communicating God's Word in a Complex World: God's Truth or Hocus Pocus?* Lanham, MD: Rowman & Littlefield, 2003.

Siyameta, Patrice M. *Return to Babel: Global Perspectives on the Bible.* Edited by Priscilla Pope-Levison and John R. Levison. Louisville: Westminster John Knox, 1999.
Sjöberg, Tore. "Giv Fredens Helige Ande!" *Evangelii Härold*, 1939.
Sjöström, Jonas. Interview on "Methodology Becoming Theology" by Phil Zarns, 2017.
Smith, James E. *The Major Prophets.* Old Testament Survey Series. Joplin, MO: College, 1992.
Söderqvist, Daniel. "Raggavagga Kakkala Raggavagga—Dn.Se." *Dagens Nyheter*, May 17, 1997.
Stephenson, William. "Introduction to Q-Methodology." *Operant Subjectivity* 17/ 1/2 (October 1993) 1–13.
Stiernstedt, Jenny. "'10 År i Sverige Utan att ha lärt sig Svenska—Då är något fel.'" *Svenska Dagbladet*, July 6, 2016.
Strong, James. *Strong's Exhaustive Concordance of the Bible.* Peabody, MA: Hendrickson, 2007.
Stronstad, Roger. *The Charismatic Theology of St. Luke: Trajectories from the Old Testament to Luke-Acts.* Edited by Mark Powell. Grand Rapids: Baker, 2012.
Sturmark, Christer. "Debattartikel: 'Grattis Till Dig Som Funderar På Att Lämna Svenska Kyrkan!'" *Sveriges Television*, February 28, 2017.
Svenska Kyrkan. "Historik." 2016. https://www.svenskakyrkan.se/656230.
———. *Inträden i och Utträden ur Svenska Kyrkan år 1970–2014.* Uppsala, Sweden: Svenska Kyrkan, 2014.
———. "Vårt Arbete." https://www.svenskakyrkan.se/vart-arbete.
Swanson, James, and Orville Nave. *New Nave's Topical Bible.* Oak Harbor, WA: Logos, 1994.
Swedish Institute. "10 Fundamentals of Religion in Sweden." https://sweden.se/society/10-fundamentals-of-religion-in-sweden/.
Tamez, Elsa. *Return to Babel: Global Perspectives on the Bible.* Edited by Priscilla Pope-Levison and John R. Levison. Louisville: Westminster John Knox, 1999.
Taylor, Charles. *A Secular Age.* Cambridge, MA: Harvard University Press, 2007.
Teasley, Daniel O. "Helgelse." *Evangelii Trumpet*, 1907, 2.
Thomas, Robert L. *New American Standard Hebrew-Aramaic and Greek Dictionaries.* Updated ed. Anaheim, CA: Foundation, 1988.
Thörn, Andreas K. G. "En Framgångsrik Främling." Dissertation, Örebro Universitet, 2014.
Trägårdh, Lars. *State and Civil Society in Northern Europe: The Swedish Model Reconsidered.* Stockholm, Sweden: Berghahn, 2007.
Trägårdh, Lars. Interview on Swedish values by Phil Zarns, November 9, 2015.
Uggla, Bengt K. *Ricoeur, Hermeneutics, and Globalization.* New York: Bloomsbury, 2011.
Van Rheenen, Gailyn. *Missions: Biblical Foundations and Contemporary Strategies.* Grand Rapids: Zondervan, 2014.
Wästberg, Olle. "Sweden—a New Melting Pot?" *The Local*, December 16, 2008. http://www.thelocal.se/20081216/16394.
Watts, Simon, and Paul Stenner. *Doing Q Methodological Research: Theory, Method & Interpretation.* Thousand Oaks, CA: Sage, 2012.
Webber, Robert E. *Who Gets to Narrate the World?: Contending for the Christian Story in an Age of Rivals.* Downers Grove, IL: InterVarsity, 2009.

Weibull, Jörgen. *Swedish History in Outline*. Trelleborg, Sweden: Svenska Institutet, 1997.

Weigel, George. *The Cube and the Cathedral: Europe, America, and Politics without God*. Leominster, UK: Gracewing, 2005.

Wenell, Fredrik. *En Pentekostal Ecklesiologi För Hållbar Utvecklng* [A Pentecostal Ecclesiology for Renewable Development]. Teologi För Hela Skapelsen—Forskningsrapporter Från Institutet För Pentekostala Studier 7. Edited by Ulrik Josefsson and Magnus Wahlström. Alvik, Sweden: Pingst FFS, 2017.

Wenk, Matthias. *Community-Forming Power*. Academic paperback. New York: Bloomsbury Academic, 2004.

Wildavsky, Aaron B. *The Nursing Father: Moses as a Political Leader*. Tuscaloosa, AL: University of Alabama Press, 1984.

Wiman, Björn. "Kyrkan Är Fortfarande Vårt Största Kulturhus." *Dagens Nyheter*, May 22, 2016. http://mobil.dn.se/kultur-noje/kyrkan-ar-fortfarande-vart-storsta-kulturhus/.

WIN/Gallup. "End of Year Survey." In *Regional and Country Reports*. Zurich: Worldwide Independent Network of Market Research, 2014.

Witoszek, Nina, and Lars Trägårdh. *Culture and Crisis: The Case of Germany and Sweden*. Oxford, UK: Berghahn, 2002.

World Values Survey. "WVS Database." http://www.worldvaluessurvey.org/WVSContents.jsp.

Yates, Timothy. *Christian Mission in the Twentieth Century*. Cambridge, UK: Cambridge University Press, 1996.

Yoder, John Howard. *The Politics of Jesus: Vicit Agnus Noster*. Grand Rapids: Eerdmans, 1994.

York, John V. *Missions in the Age of the Spirit*. Edited by S.M. Horton. Springfield, MO: Gospel, 2000.

www.ingramcontent.com/pod-product-compliance
Lightning Source LLC
Chambersburg PA
CBHW071449150426
43191CB00008B/1280